Farewell Happy Fields

KATHLEEN RAINE

Farewell Happy Fields

MEMORIES OF CHILDHOOD

Farewell happy fields
Where joy for ever dwells;
PARADISE LOST

C. Ic

GEORGE
BRAZILLER

NEW YORK

Published in the United States in 1977 by George Braziller, Inc.
Copyright © 1973 by Kathleen Raine
Originally published in England by Hamish Hamilton Ltd.

Library of Congress Cataloging in Publication Data

Raine, Kathleen Jessie, 1908–
    Farewell happy fields.

Autobiography.
    1. Raine, Kathleen Jessie, 1908–   —Biog-
raphy. 2. Authors, English—20th century—Biog-
raphy. I. Title.
PR6035.A37Z52   1977   821′.9′12   76–55847
ISBN 0–8076–0859–9

Printed in the United States of America
First Printing

INTRODUCTION

'The illumination of dreamers is from
the dead, of the waking, from dream.'

W AS IT perhaps twelve years ago that I began writing down all that I then wished to preserve of my life? Dates for me do not come into that category, for the book I have written is not intended as a factual, objective record of events. I began to write at a moment when my own story seemed to have come to an end; and twelve (if it is twelve) years later this still seems to have been so, in a certain sense. But when experience ends, the understanding of what we have experienced and done, has scarcely begun; that penultimate judgement in which we are ourselves judge and accused and sole witness.

In the fragments that follow (the first section of what I then wrote—there are two more) I tell of my life to the end of childhood. What at some other time I might have recalled, and called my story, I cannot say; for we select, in retrospect, in the light of whatever present self we have become, and that self changes continually. Some new experience may reawaken a whole sequence of past memories, or some mood shed on the past its own colour. There is also a mechanical memory, but who cares for its records?

However, if in the course of time we come a little into our own, we begin to see reflected in the seemingly fortuitous succession of events the inner pattern of our own nature, of what was predestined for us through what we are. Only when it has reflected that inner order can what has befallen us be truly called our life. It may be said that we forget or falsify past events in retrospect; but the aspect seen in recol-

5

lection may be no less true than that of the present, so vivid yet so formless. Talking once with C. S. Lewis of telling the truth about one's own life (and he in several books attempted that truth on several levels) I remember his using the figure of a range of hills. When we are climbing those hills we are among the rocks, we toil up the long ascent or rest beside some mountain stream; we meet the wind, we are drenched to the skin. But from far on we look back and see a range of blue summits against the sky. Yet both, he said, are true: the blue crests on the horizon are real also.

The story we tell at one time is not the same story as we would have told, or will perhaps tell, at another. Yet the compulsion to tell our story is in itself significant; the time for telling is ripe. Or so I trust. For to alter now what I wrote then (otherwise than a little compression and a minimum of rewriting here and there) is something I feel unable to do. If I were to write the book now it would be a different book; but it would lack the living impulse of a first time; nor would it now, as then, be written from any deep inner compulsion, if only because that impulse was spent on the first composition. It would be written in cold blood, which would be worse than not writing at all. I can see the many faults in what I have made but there is no altering them now.

If in trying to give the essence of the life which it has been mine to live (and of what other life can I tell, since each of us has direct knowledge only through the self we are) I have told many things that must seem trivial, and not told of just those events and encounters that journalists would think worth telling (encounters with famous people and so on) it is because these things were extraneous to my story. Living memory selects what belongs to love, rejecting days and weeks and months and years as so much irrelevance, treasuring certain moments known only to ourselves. People claim to have 'met' or even to have 'known' us at such a time and in such a place; but we know that we were never in that place, or only as a traveller passing through on our

6

way to those times and places where life awaits us. The outward events were as irrelevant as the landscape seen from the window of a railway-train: time merely carried us through and past. The person the world may have seen has been rather a cloak of invisibility than my real presence, perhaps more so than with most people because so little of my life has been lived where I wished, or with whom I wished; so that I must often have seemed elusive and undependable. But I have felt that the enforced necessity of bodily presence need not commit the soul. I have reserved the right to be absent in spirit; and absent I have been, more often than not, on precisely those occasions when I have been 'met' or 'seen'; I have been most myself when alone.

I once somewhere read that it is a mark of the perfection of the wise to arrive at the place they should be, at the time they should come; but such correspondence does not belong to lives less perfect. If we even sometimes, momentarily, arrive at the time and the place, it is already much. The marvel is that we ever do arrive at what is our own; and then with such a sense of homecoming, as though the long waste of time stretching before and after had never existed at all. Even though what we come to as our own may not be some happy ending but a confrontation with the tragic or the terrible. There are (as Edwin Muir, in his autobiography, *The Story and the Fable*, has written) times in every life when we seem 'to be recapitulating some legendary drama which, as it has recurred a countless number of times in time, is ageless'. But what the legend may be (and this too he said) we do not know, or only partly know; a partial knowledge which drives us with compelling passion to further discovery.

Part of the Fable we know; Paradise and the Fall. And as surely as we each enact the Fall, so have we memories of Paradise. My own have been a refuge, a source of wisdom and poetry, inexhaustible to this day. They are in no way more remarkable than those of other children; but the

7

impulse to give expression to what to us has seemed beautiful or significant within that 'legendary drama', to speak of what we have loved, is in human nature and needs no justification. What is all the art and poetry of the world but the record of remembered Paradise and the lament of our exile? We tell one another, we remind one another, we seek ever to re-create, here on earth, what we saw and knew once, elsewhere and for ever.

From more than sixty years in this world in the course of which I have met many people and read innumerable books, I treasure most those intimations I have received of another, of eternity reflected in time or glimpsed between its moments. More significant than dream-like wanderings in the unreality of 'real' life have been dreams themselves; which have at times seemed epiphanies of reality itself. Those who consider 'reality' to be situated in the world of quantity will see no value in them. But what are 'real' lives but fantasies enacted, and the greatest the most fantastic? What fantasies, indeed, human beings choose to realize! Who, in any case, can distinguish between a 'real' event and what we only thought or felt it to be? 'Facts' melt away as we examine them, and their apparent materiality dissolves into thoughts, feelings, insights. What other facts are there than these? And what, for that matter, is a world but a mode of consciousness? Times and places, mountains and seas and houses and cities, all these are only the lived experience of those who inhabit them; the world is continuously woven of our thoughts: there is no other.

Find your myth, then live it, was Jung's rule of life. But how, unless by hard trial and fatal error, find the story which is ours? Or (having known, and perhaps we all do know as children, what that story is), how keep to the plot among the shifting scenery of the world, among characters noisily, or all too persuasively, enacting other stories, in which we are cast for God knows what minor (or, more fatally, major) parts, to our own undoing? And what is worse we do the same to others. That invisible gossamer thread under the finger of Macdonald's Princess—how is the lost traveller expected not to lose it down under the hill? To know what is our own and to avoid those insidious distractions—how difficult it is; and yet not quite impossible; and I at least know that I have only myself to blame when I have lost my way. From earliest childhood—since when before I could hold a pencil my mother wrote down my first poems—I have known my vocation to be that of the poet; I saw no other life as a possibility, so that I cannot in any sense say that I chose to be a poet. I have rather evaded and neglected than chosen and persevered in my allotted task.

When I showed the sections that follow to Willa Muir, she used to tell me that I am too much given to 'floating off into *anima mundi*'; bread and salt, she said, not honey-dew, is the food of life. But bread and salt—and in the present world how poor and savourless these have become—are still more easily come by than honey-dew; a trace element, perhaps, without which none of us can live. I think of the lives of Bede and Cuthbert and Plotinus, Milarepa and St. Teresa (and indeed of C. G. Jung and W. B. Yeats), woven on a weft of miracle; and regret not so much that I have only honey-dew to offer, as that I have so little. So much beauty, so many marvellous things have slipped away unrecorded. There would be time later, I have thought, assured that this moment I could never forget, this scene was for ever written on my memory. But it is not only of dreams of the night that the poet finds that 'though he still retained some vague and dim recollection of the general purport of the vision, yet, with the exception of some eight or ten scattered lines and images, all the rest had passed away like the images on the surface of a stream into which a stone has been cast, but, alas! without the after restoration of the latter.'

January 10th, 1973

9

CHAPTER ONE

O flowers,
That never will in other Climate grow

I REMEMBER, in the beginning, a place of perfect happiness, filled with the bright sun of Easter, pure living light and warmth. My place was my state and therefore in it I knew myself where it was mine to be. That was the beginning of a dream which recurred again and again in early childhood; the dream, as I now suppose, of my birth into this world.

So it always began; but I did leave that place, caught up, as it seemed, into a gentle drift as of existence unwinding itself, flowing out of the timeless state in which I still reposed as I floated along the peaceful river past beautiful fields of flowers bathed in living light. But little by little I would find myself drawn irresistibly into the flux; and as I realized that it was no longer in my power to return or to stop, I began to be afraid. The sides of the stream grew steep and dark and dangerous, then rocky cliffs towered like great walls, and then these no longer resembled nature, but a modern city. Between towering buildings I was swept along against my will, my fear increasing as I was carried towards the machines, throbbing and grinding. Down the rapid current I was plunged into a narrow passage where the machines caught me at last among their rending wheels. At this point I always awoke, in terror.

The dream was always the same; and I knew that from bliss I would plunge into terror, from the freedom of being into the power of an irresistible mechanical destruction. I also knew that the dream was my life; the pattern it would

11

follow of necessity; the substance, I might have thought, of all generated life. But in dreams we do not generalize, we experience.

A little hand of flame, blue-tipped, thin, labile, without substance or constant form, dancing gently on a gas-jet from the wall. In my warm cot gently laid to sleep I watched those luminous fingers dancing for me, for me. I found a song to rise and fall with the hand of the flame, glimmer and glum, glimmer and glum, glimmer and glum, and so on and on. The living flame was a being, strange and familiar, familiar and strange. My father would turn it out, send the little hand away.

Flowers. The pink aromatic clusters of the flowering currant bush hung over my pram. I looked up at those flowers with their minute perfect forms, their secret centres, with the delight of rapt knowledge. They were themselves that knowledge. Not discovery but recognition; recollection; not as memory brings the past to the present but as something for ever present coming to itself. In the manifold, the innumerable I AM, each flower was its own I am. A bush burning green and rose in the light of day.

There were other flowers; chickweed's slender chalices did not then seem small or insignificant, but filled my beholding as full as a rose window in a cathedral, in all their minute perfection of beautiful form.

In that garden there was a face; or rather not so much a face as a smile; a maiden's face embracing me with that smile painted ten thousand times, the smile the Virgin shines for ever into every cradle. May's long hair was golden as sunbeams seen through half-closed eye-lashes spreading the golden light into long rays. May was the little girl next door, and I loved her. The rest of her family were ugly people with loud voices. They had a little greenhouse with spiny cactuses.

12

I lived in a world of flowers, minute but inexhaustible; the wild fragrance of thyme on the moor outside my grand-father's stone garden wall filled me to the brim with itself; it was the moor and the light high air and the thrilling bird-voice on the moor. In the shade of the north wall there was a bed of mint and cool pansies I was allowed to pick; and these flower-faces looked at me, each and every one greeted me in a here and now that had no beginning and no end. All were mine, whatever I saw was mine in the very act of seeing. To see was to know, to enter into total relationship with, to participate in the essential being of each *I am*. Strange and mysterious some seemed; the little grey-dusted lichen-cups on my grandfather's stone wall, some with what seemed like scarlet eggs in a nest; jagged forms, with-out a predictable pattern, never twice the same; and yet their beauty was, again, distinctly intelligible to me, was knowledge of essential meaning which, in living form, states itself more perfectly than any words can name it. The forms of nature mean what they are, are what they mean, endlessly and for ever, and their meanings are the ever-varying expression of the one life. The language of Eden—do we share it in some measure with the animals and birds and all the conscious creatures of the earth?—may be forgotten, but it is not to be learned: it is innate knowledge, and each recognition is like a remembrance of something for ever known.

Behind my grandfather's vegetable garden was a pine-wood, a dark secret world of its own. From that pine-wood came the cock pheasant I saw standing in his living glory among the rows of peas and grey-leaved young turnip. What was he? So perfectly himself he was, with his golden eyes and his gold-brown train; he was himself to the least spreckle of his feathered breast, his small proud head observing me. The fear I felt at the otherness of his life was part delight in his beauty, part awe in the presence of his

13

touch-me-not, his 'I am that I am.' Every creature has a measure of power peculiar to itself and to its kind; I was in the presence of his bird-kind, his pheasant-kind, and the proud life that informed that feathered dress, that jewelled head and harsh beak, that deliberate gait; the absoluteness of his being there before me. I beheld and worshipped.

I remember the palpable stillness of that pine-plantation, the fir-cones lying where they fell on the carpet of needles muting sound in a place shunned by all life but that of the trees themselves, with their branches for ever dying away below to form overhead an endlessly entangled dead thicket. In my fear of its dusk was also an exultation in the experience of the wood-in-itself, as another vista of awareness into which consciousness could flow. The circumference of consciousness was the circumference of the perceptible world; the world perceived was that consciousness, that consciousness the world: there was no distinction between seer and seen, knowledge and its object. All was mine, because myself.

Perhaps those called 'nature-mystics' simply retain longer than others our normal consciousness, our birth-right, lost sooner or later, or returning only rarely; or it is we who return only rarely, and lose Eden by a turning away, a refusing to look. Our separate identity grows over us like a skin, or shroud.

Places have their identity as flowers or creatures have, their soul, or *genius loci*. A place, in nature, is, after all, only a larger and more complex organism, a symbiosis of many lives. All inviolate places have this wholeness of essence; their perfection lies in their remaining intact, undisturbed by the intrusion of any life which does not itself participate in that harmonious organic unity; the shepherd and his dog, the ploughman and his plough, but not the bull-dozer or the motor-car or the actively or passively destructive

14

presences these bring. I think of the little glen of a burn that tumbles down a series of falls into the Tyne. A path winds up beside it to the pool where the highest fall of the linn pours its fluctuating veil of water into dark turmoil. Never, in later life, do we experience that sense of perfect arrival that is, in childhood, the term of every walk; we bring the whole of ourselves to the very place, we have not already in thought moved on, or away; our thought is what we see and love and touch. We bring no ghostly memories, no pictured fantasies, with us. We are eternally there, outside time or change. That is perhaps the secret of our power of returning to certain places in memory: to places to which we never truly came, we can never return. So I call up before the mind's eye that sounding misty linn of white water falling over dripping rock, fringed with emerald liver-wort and maiden-hair and yellow pimpernel. A single noble spray of the pale blue chimney bell-flower leans and nods in the commotion of the fall. Stream and rock, tree and fern, down to the most minute frond is formed each by the whole, and the whole by each. A leaf turns here to reach the light, another is pale in the shadow; the moss advances towards moisture, the twining honeysuckle ascends to-wards the light. Rock is shaped by water, water flows as rock bars the way or makes a passage; the dark shadow of trout, their heads up-stream, fins in balance with the weight of the flow; the black slugs in their world of decay and moisture, their glossy, embossed skins as beautiful as the leathery liverwort of their habitation, the toadstool, pullulating with maggots into liquefaction, all these held within one harmony. Within that larger unity each centre of life unfolds its own unity of form in perfect and minute precision. The whole is made up not of parts but of wholes. Nature a whole made up of wholes, perfection in the most minute particle sense can pursue. The tall spray of campanula holds in balance air and water and light as these pass through it on their way; yet each bud of flower and leaf is signed with a

15

geometric form peculiar to that species and no other, down to the smallest curve of leaf-margin and the peculiar roughness of hairs on the stem. No less formally ordered is the movement of the plant through time, its two years of life from seed to decay bringing it to perfection in the month and week appointed; for the harmony of nature is in continual motion and metamorphosis, the coming and going of forms in time. The whole of organic life—the soul of nature—is engaged in nothing else but the embodiment and unfolding of forms, in all the intricate and complex delicacy of veining, colouring, feathering, spot, stripe, notch, fleck and scale: how should the creatures not in some sense know and enjoy what they are about, what, indeed, they simply are, intricate patternings and evolving forms of mathematical art? The sense of the beautiful has deep roots, it is a knowledge that is at the same time our occupation and our delight, intuitive in earliest childhood, and rooted in our very nature, in the growth in which our bodies are engaged. 'And perhaps this faculty pronounces by comparing the object with the form which the soul herself contains and using it as a basis for judging, as a rule is used to compare straightness.'

I remember, too, a little dark paved yard behind the village post office kept by a second cousin of my father's in County Durham, where a few ferns grew, and the yellow-flowered oxalis, undisturbed in their green lives, scarcely breathed on by human presence. The little secret place had the numinous quality of a sanctuary where plant-forms had composed themselves into a harmony of equilibrium, in which even the smallest moss-scale had achieved its orientation towards the great sun. As a child I learned from these minute harmonies in which every leaf and tendril is in balance with every other, and all with the light, to know when I was myself in orientation; a faculty we share with the animal and perhaps the vegetable kingdoms, but tend to

16

lose through disuse or abuse. The gift is one whose possession is in itself a source of deep happiness, when we are in our due place, but of the unease of warning when we are not—the unease which sets animals wandering and searching for a place they feel to be right for them. So women know when they are wearing the wrong clothes not by reason but by a kind of instinctive misery. I had a scarlet coat when I was four or five years old in which I experienced all the malaise of a white blackbird, and cried and protested until my mother gave up the attempt to make me wear it.

But the surface of this endlessly unfolding veil of nature is not solid. The knowledge that existence builds its beautiful forms over who knows what abyss terrified my infant soul. Fear centred upon two dangerous thin places in the texture of the world, both on the moor above my grandfather's stone house, Hollinwood, near Kielder: a bog, and a powder magazine.

Up onto the moor my father used to carry me, so I remember, wrapped in a brown plaid shawl; secure. The way passed—or is this all a fantasy woven about some trifling patch of wet ground?—between two bottomless bog-holes, treacherously mantled over with pale green sphagnum moss. To sink there was to sink out of life; mouth and nose and ears choked with black mud, I would sink down into the bottomless place. I clung to my father as we passed between those perilous mouths.

The other terror was of another kind of annihilation. Perhaps for some stone-quarry, perhaps for the outcrops of coal mined at Plashetts, there was a small stone hut, far away from every place (so it seems to memory) a house with a door but no window, where nobody lived or ever would live. There, my father told me, gunpowder was stored, for it might at any time explode and blow to pieces everything near. That is why the stone hut stood isolated

17

and shunned. Then why was gunpowder kept at all? my infant self asked; I cannot remember my father's reasonable answer to my unreasoned protest against the very fact of destruction; for the idea of violent destruction was an outrage to some essential organic creaturely sense in me. My father, whose father was a coal-miner in County Durham, would certainly not have understood that he was, in bringing to my notice so useful and powerful a thing as gunpowder (one of the tools of the miner's craft) filling me with such a sense of outrage. The moor was beautiful, for the heather and thyme, grey lichen and green grasshoppers unfolded each to its term of perfection; the place was woven of their many lives; but the blasting and shattering of rocks and earth, the uprooting of heather and tormentil, the destroying of the nests of the stonechat and the lark was a destruction of being and meaning by the meaningless. How could an activity intrinsically destructive not be evil and its agents evil? 'For since everything formless is naturally capable of receiving shape and form, in so far as it does not participate in reason and form, it is ugly and apart from the Divine Reason; and it is in this that ugliness of every sort consists.'

Yet I gathered flowers with never a thought that I was destroying them in my desires to possess them, to hold them in my hands. I loved also butterflies; and my father must have caught them for me, shown me how to catch them under his straw hat. I must now have been four or five years in the world. I had been taught that what you must do with butterflies is to kill them, then pin them on a cork, in a box, their wings outspread. They were then called specimens; and I had seen a box covered with glass, hung on the wall, filled with dead butterflies: a *collection*. My first deep betrayal was to kill the butterflies; Red Admiral, Tortoiseshell, Peacock butterflies from the nettles. I had been told that the way to kill them is to pinch their thorax with the

18

nails of thumb and finger. I did as I was told, unquestioningly: then I saw them with horror moving their legs slowly, but not dead; and knew what I had done.

I understand now that it is to my mother I owe the happiness of my infancy as I remember or have since imagined it. I could not have come and gone among my flowers had not her remote presence assured my freedom. She never constrained me, and to her I owed that most precious solitude in which I could lose myself. I do not remember her face or appearance then so much as certain phrases which return; of a poem by George Macdonald she used to say to me: 'Where do you come from, baby dear?/ Out of the everywhere into here.' The poetry of infancy was vivid to her. Thank God, she was a poetic mother, not a practical one. To the baby in her pram how early she communicated her own sense of the mystery and beauty of the earth.

Doubtless it was from her I inherited my love of wandering the moors; for not so long before my birth she had herself been the young girl who among that same heather recited to the winds *Comus* and *Samson Agonistes*, of which she knew all, and *Paradise Lost*, of which she knew most by heart. Yet it was not the freedom of Paradise but a first foretaste of exile that first awakened the poetic instinct in me; the first intimation of a beauty inaccessible. In my infancy the pattern of my life was already indelibly drawn; there began my longing for that legendary land which some call Eden, some Erin, some Zion, some Tibet; I called it Scotland.

From Scotland my people had come, my mother's people; for my father's people were never my people, in any living sense. Scotland is to this day a matriarchal country, and my mother's family naturally regarded me as my mother's daughter rather than my father's. My father, besides, had no continuity of tradition to pass on; if from my mother's side I inherited however small a portion in the memories of

19

Scotland embodied in song, speech, and heroic story my father stood for progress, education and the future. These two influences formed me; but if I am grateful for the education to which I was subjected by my father, it is because it has given me that sad knowledge of 'good lost, and evil won', and the words in which to lament the destruction of tradition by education; for my maternal inheritance is too far away from me, too meagre for me to have preserved more than its shadow and the sense of its loss. Yet far as I have been carried from my origins, meagre as was my inheritance, the poet in me is my mother's daughter, and owes more to that lost birthright than to all the extraneous book learning I have since acquired.

The Cheviots were the hills to which (in words then familiar, for the learning by heart of the psalms was no less a part of childhood than the hills themselves) I lifted mine eyes; from them came my help. To this day a range of distant hills is to me like a promise of paradise. Beyond those hills, so they told me, lay Scotland, 'over the Border'; our own country. Displacement was already my inheritance, but by so small a distance that I could still see the country to which (so I was given to understand, not in so many words but by a thousand expressions of that profound love of a native place which among country people is as strong, perhaps stronger, than the love of persons) we belonged.

My mother's mother was a native of Edinburgh; of her people I know nothing except that an aunt who kept a dame's school had been a friend of Mr. Gladstone, who called her the most intelligent woman he had ever known. Whether that was a compliment I do not know. There was some remote kinship too with the Adam brothers, the architects of Edinburgh.

A great-grandmother, remembered by my mother, was called O'Hara, and smoked a pipe, kept secretly in a box which my mother was sometimes asked to bring her, with warnings not to look inside. My grandfather came from Forfar; from his father he had inherited his skill in fly-fishing, his knowledge of Milton's poetry, and his addiction to whisky. Was it the songs, sung not as songs learned, but as if the spontaneous utterance of some immediate feeling, or as the telling of our own story, that so early gave me the sense of identity within the tradition of Scotland? Or that speech, with some qualitative implication of feeling in every noun and verb, so fitted to express the life I myself knew, of open moor and sheltered barn, of cow-byre and kitchen, sweet Maiden's Blush roses blooming in the shelter of stone walls, a poverty redeemed by a natural setting both noble and free, fine and delicate, of a consciousness, a knowledge indistinguishable and inseparable from a country of hills and mountains and streams, of bird and blossom. In my infancy the resolution to go straight back to my true native land was pure and passionate; little did I then know the great distance of that journey back. So near the Border, all that was to be loved and desired, all of which the songs told, seemed to be not quite out of reach, near enough to arouse and to betray hope continually. I see nothing arbitrary in the process by which our lives at every moment give us symbols appropriate to what we are; and to say that imagination is 'conditioned' by an accident of geography seems to me quite inadequate as an account of the journey of consciousness through the ever-changing landscape of a life. It may be the other way round, and the scene set by imagination itself.

The sense of living as an exile in a foreign land, of being of another race and kind from those among whom I have lived, has not weakened to this day, so deeply was it implanted in me, in my infancy, by my mother's kin; they themselves already exiles, though living only a few miles over the English border, but as race-proud aliens in an alien land.

Yet my infancy and childhood had 'one foot in Eden' in

a sense more than symbolic: we were to the north of Hadrian's wall, in *Scotia irridenta*; beyond the reach of the imposed law of the Romans, on the side of the unconquered people. Here the legendary Picts had defended our sanctuary against servitude and civilization; and there I felt myself to belong with the untamed creatures of the wild sanctuaries of whom the songs of Scotland tell, with deer and curlew and lapwing of the moor, not to the trammelled history of civilization. Yet living as we did south of the modern frontier (an invisible one, however, less majestic and ancient than that wall I later knew well, whose hewn stones, whose fosse and vallum, sometimes lost, yet so persistently reappear, running on and on, from Corbridge and Chollerford over the Nine Nicks, bare moor and crag farther than eye can follow) we were nevertheless in some sense excluded. I did not know what those mysterious frontiers were that lay between my world and the country of the poems and the ballads. The place of poetry seemed to me, then, a place in this world, of this world, and only a few miles away.

The place I was later and for years to come to love most in the world was within sight of the Green Rigg where the Douglas had died under the same tall bracken that was higher than my head when at last I climbed its slope. There was a loch, and a crag called 'the old Man of the Wannies' because its rocky fall had the profile of a man's face; and a pair of ravens (the last in England, it was said, though this may have been a poetic more than a literal truth) nested there. But before I ever saw that place, 'the wild hills o'Wannie', a line perhaps from some poem by a local bard, spoken by my Aunty Peggy Black in her sweet treble, was as the ʽεις ʽοροϛ in *The Bacchae*, a summons to that other world. It was the phrase itself which acted on me as a spell: *wild hills*; and they were there, visible far away, where my Aunty Peggy pointed. The phrase named those hills as a place not in the world so much as in the poem; promised

in that very place the wildness-in-itself of all hills. I had only
to reach the Wannies to be in that essential world.

So it was that at last, one day, one fair northern summer's day, we set out, my mother, my Aunty Peggy and my
infant self in my little push-car. We crossed the farmyard
with its scent of camomile and cow-dung, and through the
one of its several gates which opened upon the high bare
pasture where the peewits are always wheeling over the
outcrop of rock where they nest, their high domain, set out
towards the wild hills. We were already above the level of
trees, and as we climbed the turf became finer and softer,
with wild pink and wild thyme and rock-rose. We came to
the little crag where in the warren there were always a few
black rabbits among the brown—I knew the place well later.
Wild it seemed, without wall or man-made road, the
creatures wild in the rocks, and far and wide. Was this 'the
Wild Hills o'Wannie'? No, I was told, farther on, could I not
see them in the distance? And there—so memory has composed the picture, or imagination has—the sun was setting
their crests on fire with gold, and we were walking along the
green road of the long summer day towards those bright
hills until it seemed to me I could see the purple of the
heather on their slopes. We were on our way, we were going
to the place itself.

Until we came to the farm of Sweethope, where my
mother and aunt were merely going to take tea with the
farmer's wife and daughters. Would we go on after tea to the
Wild Hills o'Wannie? Oh yes, after tea; be a good girl and
wait; and after tea we walked long in the garden among the
phloxes and sweet peas and the late summer flowers. I must
have given a good deal of trouble, for not for one moment
did I relinquish my quest, or realize that this was the end
and not the beginning of that for which we had come. The
fair promises had all been a ruse to keep a baby happy on a
walk across those long Northumbrian pastures.

After tea in my push-car I was again happy: we were
23

setting off, at last, for those beautiful hills; but the push-car was turned round towards home, myself crying and struggling. They promised that I should go there 'someday'—that beautiful horizon of time, where as upon mountains distant in space, resides that same imagined beauty. They thought I would forget, as soon as they themselves, my purpose to go to that place; but I was, on that day, not the baby in the push-car but the self I was later to become, or already was. At last poetry came to my aid, and I fell into a chant, repeating the magic phrase over and over until the words became a sort of mantra. 'I want to go to the wild hills o'Wannie.' By incantation I tried to bring near the far bright beauty of the hills. In need of magic for so specific an end I discovered the use of poetry.

I later learned that not only were there certain places which belonged to that world of which poetry tells, but also certain animals, and birds. The hawk, the heron and the raven, appearing in all the power of their magical significance, would write across the sky some word of ill-omen or of splendour. To see the heron, or the crow, was, in that remote world, an epiphany of indescribable mystery; not the mystery merely of the bird itself (though that was part of it) but of something which concerned also the seer of the bird, a confluence of our existence with the existence of the bird and of both with something else otherwise inexpressible. This was something more than a child's *participation mystique*, it was a mode of knowledge communicated to me by my elders in the tone of voice in which it would be said 'there is the heron'—or the corbie, or the hawk—it was always 'the', not 'a', for any individual bird or beast was as if endowed with the full identity of all its kind. (Such lowly creatures as rabbits were not so distinguished by the definite article, but were only named by the collective form, or the plural.) We felt, I think, that the bird itself knew that which to us it communicated. Thus the corbie was 'an evil bird',

24

condemned by us for that dark nature of which it told, as if a conscious agent. But to put it so is to translate—and how inadequately—into the language of words what was itself a language far more powerful and no less exact; a language in which bird and beast and tree were themselves the words, full of otherwise inexpressible meaning. Poetry was not then words on the page, but birds in the air, in the dusk, against the wind in the high blue air; it was trees, it was stones and springs, an ever-changing face of things which communicated knowledge words can only remotely capture or evoke.

To that order also belonged certain people; and with these people, belonging as they did to the world imagination seeks always to enter, I felt some deep link. The old hierarchic society had subtle virtues for the imagination, most of all perhaps for those who had least to gain in material terms from the caste system. Imagination loves nobility and splendour and tragedy and beauty and kingship; loves all great things; of equality, that doctrinaire abstraction, it knows nothing. It is very likely that our neighbouring Armstrongs and Shaftos and Douglases or even the Percys themselves no longer participated in the living tradition which for their tenants they continued to embody, bearing as they did names from those ballads which were our sole cultural heritage long after they had ceased to be theirs. Doubtless education had brought them into the twentieth century while their tenants continued to live on in legendary time; yet they continued to nourish our imagination, as those Guermantes whom Marcel was later to meet in Paris had existed for him, as a child and a young man, with another kind of reality, of which social status is itself only an image, a metaphor.

My mother's family inherited, however tenuously, the archaic attitude of the clan towards its chieftain. It is forgotten in these envious egalitarian days the extent to which the cement of such relationships was neither the compulsion of tyranny nor of economics, but imagination. It was at its roots a blood-kinship, or, what is almost as strong, a kinship through a common love of the land, of the same mountain and river, the same fields, the same prevailing wind and the sun and the stars rising and setting beyond certain abiding hills. There is a sense in which each creature possesses its world far more real than the mere token ownership conveyed by deed of property. 'That all the world is yours, your very senses and the inclination of your mind declare.' Clothed with the heavens and crowned with the stars, each creature is 'the sole heir of the whole world, and more than so, because men are in it who are every one sole heirs as well as you'. Every child knows this; and country people who, enjoying the beauty of some tree or the flowers that grow by the side of the road, are not troubled by thoughts of ownership. There is a kinship of Eden itself among all who are in Traherne's sense co-heirs of the same parcel of earth and sky. In the present world it must seem incredible that, in that old unbroken pattern, envy played no part.

There is, besides, a kind of being 'in love' with those who often bear the names, and are from legendary time associated with such enduring and continuous places. Bearing those names they embodied, in some measure, the sense of identity of the nameless people of their land, with its intangible heritage of imaginative riches. Their lives possessed a dimension which common mankind lacked, the dimension of tradition, of poetry; yet they were at the same time extensions of the lives of their nameless tenantry. No lords can so much speak of 'their' tenantry as the tenants of 'their' lords and ladies; for no economic bond has in it the immortal quality of the instinct for poetry. The names written in 'the book of the people' are not those who have done most 'good', or worked in 'the people's' cause, but those whose stories have the most poetry in them, the most of the human qualities all possess but not all can realize; the 'black' Armstrongs and Douglases, the bride-stealers and child-murderers and fratricides, the vanquished no less than the victors on legendary battle-fields.

Song and legend were a birthright which to the poorest lent the dignity of an identity conferred by ancestral participation. What are the legendary rivers of epic and ballad to strangers? Academic scholarship does not so much inherit as usurp and obliterate the living tradition it replaces. By her speech and her music, Scotland, like Ireland, had kept, even to my childhood (though not unimpaired) her imaginative identity; and my mother's share, small as it was, in this birthright, is the only inheritance I ever had. I learned with love the words of the Scottish speech, because these were 'our' words.

My father spoke 'educated' English, learned as a foreign language at Durham University, and acquired by the help of his fine fastidious ear. But my mother's family spoke 'braid Scots' bringing out, in moods of excitement, whether of tenderness or scorn, uncouth words like treasured heirlooms; for the words of a living dialect are not abstract terms, they are an imaginative map of a country of the imagination, and of experience, feelings and perceptions inseparable from experiences in, and of, that world, caught up into regions of consciousness, with the peculiar light and climate of the place. The words are concrete as if the landscape itself had uttered them; 'In behint yon auld fail dyke' can no more be translated as 'close behind that old turf wall' than can 'corbie' as 'crow'; for the words bring with them the context of their world, are inseparable from that total experience. The words of the ballad evoke an expanse of treeless moor, and lichened stone, where the harsh dialogue of 'twa corbies' is carried on the delicate air over miles of bare hillside to the ears of those who themselves participate in that total consciousness of which landscape and language are alike regions. Nor can those regions be entered by visiting the geographical site: Tweed and Till,

Sweet Afton and Flodden Field are regions which cannot, in that sense, be visited.

Now that I speak only a well-learned acquired Cambridge English I wonder if any other kind of poetry is possible than one so rooted in the unbroken continuity of language and place; a language which itself transposes into words that earlier, more richly meaningful language of bird and weather and hill, inseparable from the people who created it, and the continuity of a culture in the places named by speech. When Indians (for instance) send me poems written in what they take to be the English language, I invariably ask them why they use it; and I have never heard again from any Indian to whom I have put that question: for had they understood the answer they would not have been writing English in any case. Yet I am no better myself; an exile, even linguistically, looking back with nostalgia into a world to which in infancy I thought I belonged, but from which my people had already travelled too far for return to be possible, even for themselves, far less for me.

So it was useless for my father to oppose the doctrinaire abstractions of socialism (for he came from the world of the dispossessed who hated and envied those who inherited their place and portion in the old social order, the dispossessed already bent on its destruction) or the alien themes of 'education' to the flow of talk in the kitchen of Hollinwood; of the Duke, of the proud Duchess, of the young Earl Percy whose life was ruined through family pride, who died young, killed in a duel in France, so it was said, romantic Byronic victim of a broken heart and the legendary proud mother of the ballads who counselled her son against his true-love. There was Lord James, fair-haired as the young lords of border history, who died tragically young, and in whose sickroom his tame birds flew free; and the lady Victoria's great coils of fine-spun hair my mother had admired as she sat behind her and her sister the lady Mary in the Kielder Kirk, of the bright gold so praised in

28

ballad and song. Of all those conspicuous in our eyes as those who once walked on the Akropolis of Mycenae, the stories were woven into that unbroken thread of the memory or imagination from which Shakespeare and Homer drew only a few strands.

Such were the first stories I ever heard; and it seemed to me then as if my very identity was bound up with those stories and with the people who enacted them; figures who belonged, like the hills and rivers, to the world of my inheritance.

Was I—have I all my life been—the too much doted on child of my poetic mother, cast by her for a part not in the peasant activities of her mother's world, but in poetry? Or did I myself intuitively know that the aunts and grand-mother who pampered and bored me, the next-door-neighbours and indeed almost all the adults of my world and most of the children, were not of my kind, not con-cerned with the things which concerned me? My mother's business that I must be about? Or was it my mother's sense of innate difference, was it her inhabiting of a world whose atmosphere was freer, clearer, more wonderful than theirs, which from the beginning of my life imprinted upon me the sense that I was not of their kind? That I belonged with the golden race? For the golden race is not to be identified with class (though the class system has given it some protection) but is sown broadcast over the earth, like the wheat in the parable, to starve, or wither, or bear fruit. I was born with gifts, inherited as I now realize from my mother, and by her from her father, or perhaps merely God-given; and when I am judged it will not be for my knowledge of their posses-sion, but for the small use I have made of them. I might, I ought to have achieved more, to have left more and better poetry than I have done. How clearly childhood knew; but choked by thorns how fruitless I have been.

My Aunty Peggy Black was not my mother's sister, but

her first cousin, who had come to live with my grand-parents as an orphan at the age of ten or eleven. She was less 'educated' than my mother and her sisters, and I sup-pose of commoner clay; for it was from my handsome grandfather, who though but a village schoolmaster, knew Latin, wrote political verse-lampoons, and read aloud to his daughters (as in the evenings they sat sewing and embroider-ing—I have a patchwork quilt which my mother made in those far-off days when even the poor had leisure for such skills) the novels of Meredith and Thomas Hardy as these appeared in serial form, that my mother and her sisters inherited, along with their beauty, something rare, alto-gether out of place in the world in which they lived.

My Aunty Peggy too was a village schoolmistress, and reigned in the hamlet of Bavington; but she (not being a daughter of Alexander Wilkie) had neither beauty nor dreams to unsettle her; she was therefore at one with her world, as my mother and her sisters were not; she taught the children of farmers and hinds in her single schoolroom with its big iron stove, and its high windows, and its lobby smelling of miry clogs and carbolic soap. 'You cannot make silk purses out of sow's ears' summarized the wisdom of her years of experience with the 'gowks', 'donnarts' and 'gom-merels' who made, all the same, very good pig-skin leather in the long run. In a farming community, heredity ('like father, like son') had not, as in an egalitarian urban society in which all alike are stripped of individual qualities, been censored from the laws of nature.

It is to my Aunty Peggy Black that I owe the only years in which I was ever to know the sense—even though it was an illusory sense—of having a place on earth to which I truly belonged, and of being in that place; for in my parents' house this was never so, as will be told. How could it have been so, my mother herself living as she did as a stranger in a strange land?

My Aunty Peggy lived, at the time of my first memory,

in a two-roomed stone cottage at the top of the outcrop of rock that was our only village street. There, I remember my mother, young and full of laughter, and myself (the infant in the push-car) lifting from the earth numbers of small brown snowdrop bulbs. Perhaps the clumps were being divided, or some being given to my mother to take away. I had not known before that under the earth there were these mysterious roots of things; not shapeless like pebbles, but formed according to a pattern, and glossy and living down under the soil.

Later Aunty Peggy moved into the manse, a stone house with a big garden sheltered by beeches, and a field where the Minister had kept his pony or grown his hay, and the burn running along the bottom of the garden, its sound of swiftly running water ever my companion at night when I too lived at the manse. In that garden snowdrops were in multitude without number. After the snow they broke the ground, clumps of short green shoots tightly clasping the green edged white flower-buds stiff upright. Then a few would break their glassy sheaths and bend their graceful necks, the petals still closed; then many, then innumerable, their flowers would open, some single, some double, nestling near the house, or scattered in the half wild undergrowth down to the 'syke loning'. I can see them now in my mind's eye; but the mind's eye is a poor thing in comparison to that marvel of reality, that immaculate freshness, and the light cold early spring scent of the green-white flowers in the air fragrant after the melting of the snow. 'Ten thousand saw I at a glance', Wordsworth said of his daffodils; surely exaggerating a little. But when I think of the snowdrops in the manse garden—in the grass, under the apple-tree, cascading down towards the bordering beech trees—I see multitude as the peculiar delight of that vision. Wordsworth's ten thousand is to be read in the same sense as the 'ten thousand creatures' of Lao-Tze. That they were countless, that there were always more, gave a kind of knowledge

31

that nature is inexhaustible, that multitude is her secret, her deep mystery. There could be no end to snowdrops. When, much later I suppose, I heard of 'extinct' species, of the last of the Great Auks slaughtered on St. Kilda (with all the wild glory of Kingsley's Mother Carey's Chickens) I felt that deep sense of sorrow and outrage as at the blasting of the moor at Plashetts. For what is more 'against nature' than the killing of her creatures, the blasting of her fecundity, the erasing of one of the moulds of creation?

Bavington might itself have stood in legendary time; built of the stone of the hills, it had no age, but perfectly belonged to its place at the top of the outcrop of rock that paved the farmyard and the village street. Up and down that slope of rock, worn by clogs and hooves, came and went the dwellers in the row of three cottages below, the manse, the byre, and all who came on weekdays to the school, and Sundays to the kirk. Living in the manse, my Aunty Peggy enjoyed with the house some of the status it conferred. The school and the adjoining cottage were of great age; some said the cottage, with its mullioned windows, had formerly been part of a monastery. None who lived there had yet moved out of ancestral continuity, and the texture of their lives was inwoven with the land on which their fathers and mothers had been born before them: Hallington and Throckrington and Hare-Laws, Three Farms, and Clay Walls, and Sweethope. The texture is broken now; the children no longer walk or ride on horseback over the moorland pasture to the village school (belonging, with barn and byre and kirk to that world to which each was sole heir) but are driven away in buses to the nearest town, or the farmers' sons sent to public schools, there to lose, in exchange for education, that sense of identity with a place (which I and my own school-fellows were, I suppose, among the last to know) which belongs only to people of intact inheritance.

Bavington's 'time immemorial' can, of course, be given dates. The little Presbyterian church bears the date of its

32

building—1725; records of a congregation go back to 1662 and the times of the Covenanters. The manse was built in 1855, when the earlier manse (contemporary I suppose with the church) became 'a respectable school in which the highest branches of education' were taught. The school's founder (the Rev. Mr. Forsyth) wished 'to make the Institution of such a character as should induce the wealthy farmers and graziers of the neighbourhood to send their children to it instead of sending them to boarding-schools to finish their education'. Mr. Forsyth went personally to Scotland (for where else would a Border Minister look for a sound dominie?) to search for a teacher of 'superior qualifications'; and whether because of the excellence of the school, or because farmers had at that time little regard for book-learning, the wealthy farmers and graziers did indeed continue to send their sons and daughters to be licked into more or less silky purses by my Aunty Peggy Black, herself a native of Edinburgh.

As for the manse itself, the *Morpeth Herald* in June 1855 described it as 'neat and chaste in design, substantial in structure, and commodious in its arrangements'. In honour of its completion, a social entertainment, or a "house-warming", was held. The tea-tables, sumptuously furnished by the ladies of the congregation, were laid out in the several rooms, and crowded with a large and respectable assemblage of guests, consisting of the members of the congregation and their friends from different quarters. The utmost hilarity prevailed on this occasion. The draught "which cheers but not inebriates" was copiously supplied—and its accompaniments reflected great credit on the taste and liberality of the entertainers.' (This I can well believe; the cookery book issued on the 200th anniversary, 'which took the form of a sale of work, tea and concert' and on which occasion Miss Black's name appears among the Robsons, Waltons, Slessors, Fenwicks, Patersons, Carrs, Browells, Scotts and Bells, contains recipes for those cakes I myself remember and whose like could not now be obtained at Fortnum and Mason's.) 'In the evening the party withdrew to the Church, when they were successively addressed in very interesting speeches by the Revs. A. Forsyth, the Minister of Bavington; Fergus, Thropton; Anderson, Morpeth; Cathcart, Harbottle; Wrightson, Wark; and Lennie, Glanton.' That innocent merry-making must have left something of its sweetness in those familiar rooms that even now I so often revisit (strangely altered as they always are, but still and for ever the place of my homecoming) in nightly dreams.

The housewarming, with its six addresses, must indeed have been a grand occasion; but later members of the congegation and their friends from different quarters were always ready to attend and to enjoy, with sober hilarity, those permitted festivals, a sale of work, or a whist-drive and social. Those of us pupils at the school with the best handwriting (copperplate as it still was) would copy some dozen or more announcements of the event to be held in aid of Bavington Church on such a day; and these were nailed to certain gate-posts where they could not fail to be seen by the farmers, rich graziers, etc., and their wives; who would arrive in their traps on the day appointed to partake, in the school and the manse, of the cup that cheers, and its accompaniments of sponge-cakes, 'melting moments', singin' hinnies, gingerbread, sultana cakes, and pasties made of the fruits of every tree in the garden.

When last I saw Bavington the texture of woven and interwoven lives which had made it, in the human sense, a place, had been destroyed; the school was a youth-hostel, George Carr the school caretaker its warden; weekenders from Newcastle occupied the cottages; the retired schoolmistress who at that time occupied the manse (where the two silver Cromwellian communion-cups and the six 'tokens' had been treasured in a cupboard with deep idolatrous reverence) was 'a Roman Catholic'. All was in confusion and decline. Yet we were the first unwitting agents of the process of change; for it was my Aunty Peggy Black herself who brought to Bavington its first motor-car, and I whose task it was to open and shut the five-barred gates across the grass roads over those high moorland pastures, and to move in order to do so (along with their clouds of flies) the five or six ruminating steers or heifers which would be lying on the sun-warmed outcrop. There were some five gates between Bavington and the main road to Newcastle; they guarded the magic, the *genius loci*, such as it was; but no gates can prevail against the encroachment of the machine age which obliterates all that has unique identity.

Yet Bavington, as I remember it, seems to have stood outside the mill-race of history, abiding still within the covenant of God, 'While the earth remaineth, seed-time and harvest, cold and heat, and summer and winter, shall not cease.' Time was cyclic, not linear.

The experience of each season was, in that distant world, like a change of consciousness; and it was winter especially which then had the power to remove every farm and hamlet from common time, bringing healing isolation as its most delicate secret. The arrival of winter had a grandeur, as of the approach of that God 'who maketh the clouds his chariot: who walketh upon the wings of the wind', and whose breath comes out of the north. It was in terms of the grandeur of the God of the Psalms, of Isaiah and of Job (whose Word we gathered to hear every Sunday, read by the Minister in the little church, and whose memorizing was my Sunday task) that I saw the elements unloosed upon us, snow-clouds on the North wind that travelled unhindered over the sweep of the moors. Because of their greatness, and because they were the vehicles of God, I rejoiced in the arrival of storm, wind, snow, frost and thunder. These were attributes of the divine majesty, and the coming of a great storm the approach of the God who 'did fly upon the wings of the wind'; a dignity conferred upon our high lonely house as by the progress of the Elohim.

We knew of the approaching snow-storm not from any weather-report but from watching the 'weather-airt' of our own sky. Aunty Peggy would close the school early to let her twenty or thirty pupils get home to their remote farms in safety; she and I had only to cross from the school to the manse; we used the door through the back-kitchen, where the iron pans, soot-encrusted, in which we boiled the porridge, the potatoes and the broth, the coal-shovel, the water-dipper, the ash-riddle and the zinc pails all seemed to have grown inimical, emanating an icy coldness that clung to the skin like fire. Many years it is since I have known, as then, the ordeal of the body which winter brought, feet frozen and leaden in heavy clogs and hands stiff and red in gloves with holes in the fingers, miserably comfortless. Last thing at night when all the tasks were over, my Aunty Peggy and I would draw up our chairs to the kitchen range (where the kettle hung on its hook over the fire, and the steel dampers of the oven shone spotless at all times) to thaw out the cold of the day, the wind rattling and battering at the shutters, and the voices of the air howling as the smoke blew in gusts down the chimney. Yet these ordeals of winter seemed to raise us towards the grandeur of those elements visiting with their presences our remote hamlet.

No room was ever so cold as the blue bedroom of the manse on a January night; but the feather-bed of that icy bedroom was my refuge and my only hope of ultimate comfort from the misery of having a body in winter; when after what seemed like hours I would venture, little by little, to thaw those frozen feet against warmer parts of my small shivering body, and a glow of warmth would come at last. In the night the wind drops and I wake to the silence, a stillness as intense as the sound it replaces. The tinkle of the little burn at the foot of the garden is muted and muffled;

and the light is white, reflected back from the transfigured earth to the grey sky. Immaculate snow on garden and moor, on the tops of the dykes, on the window-sills, all is drifted into lovely and simple curves, hollows and ridges the shape of wind, the shape of eddies of wind, of gusts, and long smooth sweeping waves of wind. The wind is a subtle mathematician, a Platonist impressing on the snow an image of invisible forms ruled by number and geometry. The house, sealed by drifts of snow, its doors and windows softly barred by mysterious barricades of myriads of delicate crystals, seems removed during the night into another mode of being. Our solitude seems to set upon us some seal, as chosen and set apart by the snow, the snow-clouds and the sky, in their sanctuary. All within safe from all without, nothing the heart loved could spill or flow away. The white cups and plates, with their pattern of a gold circle and a clover-leaf; the eggs in a bowl, the loaves in the bread-crock, the paraffin-drum in the back-kitchen, the lamps, the clock on the wall, the magenta bells of the Christmas-cactus, the empty rooms of the house itself, purged of all invasive and obliterating and blurring irrelevances; space and time no longer flowing away all round them, stood in their own principle, their absolute identity. All I loved in the world was in that place, encirlced within that white horizon.

I wished that our sanctuary could remain for ever within its white barrier; but soon came Grannie Carr, a woollen cap on her toothless head, strong as ten old women, making her way in her clogs through the drifts to see how we fared; and presently George Carr would come and dig us out, baring a raw path to the door of the back-kitchen. But if the innermost sanctuary was now destroyed, another magic circle remained intact about our little hamlet; which had, overnight, drifted away from Northumberland, England, the world, into its own sphere of separate time and space. Our lives, so implicated one with another, came into a completeness. We travel in search of experience, yet nothing so

37

enhances the real as remaining in one place; and when our frontiers were closed, all humanity seemed sufficiently represented by Granny Carr and George, and George's wife Annie, and Annie's baby Francis; by old Maggie who lived in the two-roomed cottage where she raised young turkeys in a barrel turned on its side, and kept a box of 'Dainty Dinahs' and bulls-eyes to sell to the children at the school; by the unshaven farmer and his slatternly wife, with their unbroken row of annual boys, ending with a baby girl, Minnie; all their heads, cropped with the sheep-shears, patched with ring-worm and their corduroy clothes smelling of milk and cow-dung. The vague figures of the butcher, the grocer, the post, the coal, Mr. Howatson the Minister, the invasive distant world, none of these could reach us. There would be no school until the thaw, no doing sums on slates with squeaky slate-pencils, no dreamy chanting of the multiplication-tables and the rivers of England; no learning by heart of *The Revenge* or *The Lay of the Last Minstrel*, or how Horatius kept the Bridge across the Tiber, no clatter of desks and clogs as a score of children sat down after reciting the Lord's Prayer (hands together, eyes closed) in broad dialect as ancient as the boundaries of their fathers' fields; no washing of hands in school wash-basins. or comparing of warts as we dried them all together on the rough linen roller towels before the children from distant farms gathered round the great iron stove to eat the huge pasties they brought for dinner. Until the thaw, all that hum of life and effort of learning was over.

The farmyard had become a labyrinth with passages cut between walls of snow, from house to byre, from byre to barn. I wished those walls would stand for ever, and the world they so briefly and marvellously built, so strangely unlike the familiar farmyard with its outcrop of rock streaming with mud ('clart', we called it) and fragrant with camomile. Of course it ended; and perhaps it was very brief, though now it seems without beginning and without end, that condition I have tried to describe in which each thing, as if unique and altogether itself, attained its full identity in a timeless state. You can find that experience, once winter's most delicate secret, only in pictures like those painted a thousand years ago by Chinese sages whose magic brushes were able to express at once the great emptiness, and the eternal existence of every frozen twig and dry grass-stalk.

One of the foundations of my happiness in that vanished world was the security of a life in which children as a matter of course helped in the work of the day. All my school-fellows returned home, the boys to feed the beasts, the girls to milk and bake and gather eggs or pick gooseberries; and in hay-time all helped to gather the hay into pike and stook and cock. There were not two worlds, one for children and another for adults; nor for adults two worlds, one of work and one of leisure. There still remained, in the country, the integrity of that ancient way of life in which work, and whatever pleasures we might find or invent, were woven into one texture. If at times the tasks laid upon our childhood seemed hard, we had in performing them the sense of participating in the real world, whose wholeness embraced all within the horizon our eyes saw, crag and pasture, byre and garden and kitchen. Extraneous knowledge (how Horatius kept the bridge) occupied a place in our lives relatively small and quite unimportant. The poetry of life lay at hand, as in country gardens clumps of double daffodils bordered the rows of early potatoes and winter kale. We took our pleasures as we came and went upon our tasks; we were at once occupied and free, nor could we have said where tasks ended and pleasures began. We could enjoy our Maiden's Blush roses as we picked the gooseberries; and who can say whether gathering raspberries or seeking eggs be work or play? As for 'education', 'school' was not in those days seen as 'work', but rather as a respite from the hard tasks of life, which lay at home. To write a good copperplate hand was an accomplishment rather than a necessity; and who, once school was over would ever again need to recite by rote the rivers of England? Yet we did learn the structure of language, to parse and analyse sentences, to spell, and to know what were called 'Latin roots' with a thoroughness that has served me well in a life undreamed-of at Bavington school. The great virtue of that outmoded education—and that surely for all of us—was the number of poems, psalms, and passages from the Bible we learned by heart. Memory makes our own the words of power in a manner far more complete than the mere reading of them, or the knowledge of where we may look them up on our shelves. My Aunty Peggy's tastes were for rousing heroic narrative—the *Lays of Ancient Rome*, *The Burial of Sir John Moore at Corunna*, or *Nobly, Nobly Cape St. Vincent / To the north-west died away*, or *The Revenge*. My own preferences—though I learned all these, and with them the simple heroic values they express—were not ballads of tragic love (*Fair Helen* or *Lord Ullin's Daughter*, and still less *The Bridge of Sighs*) but the simple nostalgia of 'I remember, I remember / The house where I was born', and Cowper's *Poplar Field*, and 'My Heart's in the Highlands, my heart is not here'; imperceptibly leading, by way of 'He has gone from the mountain / He is lost to the forest', and 'The harp that once in Tara's Halls' to the exultant war-songs of Scotland, 'Scots wha hae wi' Wallace bled' and *The Gathering Song of Donald Dhu*. To childhood patriotism is innate, for places are more dear than people; and there is no deeper love than that given once and for ever to the place on earth which childhood held dear.

The poems of Burns and Thomas Moore I knew as songs not poems; as they are meant to be known. With some surprise I find, as I write, calling up from the long past forgotten lines, and with them the emotion they first aroused in me, that these are the poems that still have the power to move me to tears; while I can read dry-eyed all the canon of English Romantic, Metaphysical and philosophic poetry I have since studied. It is these older strata that made me whatever I am.

Among my daily tasks at the manse was the carrying of the water. The soft-water barrel stood behind the back kitchen, on the sunless end of the house, where the beautiful green liverwort, whose strange and mysterious indusia filled me with a kind of learned botanical awe, advanced over the naked rock. As I lowered the dipper into the water the larvae of mosquitoes which, undisturbed, hung as if suspended from the surface, would dive wriggling into the gloomy wooden depths. A few of these creatures, or their sloughed integuments, whose exquisite fragile delicacy of form fascinated as it repelled, found their way into my dipper with the inexorability of the laws of probability (so many to the cubic foot—I could not cheat chance) sooner or later to be poured out of the bedroom jug, their reappearance a kind of malevolent pursuit, like Pandora's troubles. There even one of them produced a scunner which marred the luxury of feeling the softness of that water (mellowed with brown fragrant Pears' soap) as I washed my hands and face in the bedroom wash-basin.

Our drinking-water I had to bring from the well in the farmyard; a task which burdened me to the extreme limit of my strength but whose imaginative delight was of a quality to which I find it difficult to give a name, for it seemed to touch springs of thought at that time unknown to me; and not altogether (like my daily delight in nature) something childhood may share with the animal creation. I took with me the tin dipper, and two buckets, held apart by a square wooden frame which prevented them from jolting and spilling against my thin young legs in their black woollen stockings. Empty they were no burden, but full, the handles of the pails cut into my hands and their weight dragged at my shoulders, so that I had to set them down more than once between the well and the water-crocks in the manse larder, under the cold stone slabs on which stood

41

the pats of butter and the bowls of milk set for the cream to rise (to be skimmed delicately with a spoon into a glass cream-jug for tea). To drink that well-water, cold and clear, was a kind of austere luxury, almost a rite; my Aunty Peggy never failed to praise, as she drank it, the water from that well as the best she had ever known; as people praise wine. Years later, in the Highlands, I again met country people who spoke of the water of their wells and springs in that ancient way as in the Book of Kings ('Give me to drink of the water of the well of Bethlehem ...'), or in Greek mythology.

The well must I think have been very old; the roughly-hewn well-head which covered the spring might have dated from the forgotten monastery; and simple as it was it spoke a language entirely strange to me at that time, not of nature, but of a different kind of meaning, which I recognized because this primitive shrine (for the well had, for me, a kind of numinosity) was raised upon a marvel of nature itself whose magic it served to enhance. I shared, as I drew my water, the wonder of those who had built the well-head, recognizing in it the expression of a mind for which, as for my own, a spring was something pure, mysterious, more than natural. The spring was not deep, and I could plunge my arm to the depth of the sand-grains which danced on the bottom perpetually, as the cold clear water welled up. This perpetual welling up of the water was to me a marvel, that emergence from the rocky darkness where water has a secret life of its own, profound, flowing in underground streams and hollows under the hills which none can know or enter. It was as if at this spot a mystery were perpetually enacted. If I found in the stone basin leaves or water-shrimps I removed them as from a sacred source.

The sense of sacred places, natural shrines, was strong in me (the Covenanters notwithstanding); one such I had made for myself on a rock upon a certain crag, where I used

42

to sit, remote as a hare on its form, looking out over the moors to the edge of the sky in a kind of religious ecstasy. I felt I ought to take there that simple symbol of the divine, my Bible, but, finding that the book did not fit the genius of the place at all, I took it home again, replacing it with treasures of my own, banded snail-shells and the like. That was my first, but by no means my last, unsuccessful attempt to attune the reality of my experience with accepted modes of religious expression. Child of nature that I was, I perhaps grew up too long without access to civilization. But I would have well understood those Buddhist stories which tell that the most sacred scriptures are the unwritten pages, an old pine-tree gnarled by wind and weather or a skein of geese flying across the sky.

Yet once it had left the well-head the little trickling stream which overflowed continually did not seem to me in any way sacred or mysterious. In it paddled the farm-yard ducks and geese, and a few yards below the well it gathered into a small muddy pond where the beasts drank. From the pond the water ran on, through the bull-field and under the high stone wall of the manse garden, swiftly running between abundant banks of saxifrage, under the luxuriant black-currant bushes which love cool moisture, through the manse hay-field and across the 'syke loning' to which it gave its name. Two fields away its waters were still pure enough for water-cress to thrive in abundance, whose dark fresh leaves I often gathered for our tea, to eat with our homemade bread, and salt; and there were wild flowers, water-avons, brooklime speedwell, marsh-marigold and many more I then knew, before the Bavington burn joined the Wansbeck, somewhere beyond our world.

The water was my morning task; and after school I fetched the evening milk, from Clay Walls, two fields away from the manse, the enamel milk-can swinging and jolting on its wire handle, the milk splashing into the inverted cup which formed its lid. Sometimes when Grannie Carr's cow

43

was in milk I was allowed to milk her, squeezing the white jet from the rough udders of life; something I did not (strangely enough, perhaps) find magical, as the well was magical, perhaps because the cow's udders were so like my own body, only coarser, and not very clean.

Sometimes Grannie Carr would take me into her parlour, there to show me her treasures—a set of biscuit-coloured Wedgwood dessert plates, and fern-leaves shaped into jugs and other forms; these I knew to be of incalculable value, something altogether of another world than ours; for Grannie Carr was an illegitimate daughter of the gentry, and the Wedgwood came from that mother, who, even even after she had been married off to a groom, kept certain standards which Grannie Carr inherited and prided herself upon: always polishing the soles as well as the uppers of shoes was one grain of gentility which had survived all these intangibles which cannot survive in an illiterate world. The Wedgwood plates I thought beautiful because they were like real ferns and leaves; but also because of their almost legendary origin, and the value set upon them as treasures once of ladies of the Hall.

In the manse kitchen I would find, on my return, the day's work over, my Aunty Peggy (whom I identified in my own mind with Ellen's upright but severe aunt in *The Wide Wide World* and Marilla of *Rebecca of Sunnybrook Farm*, my favourite books at the time, both held in high regard in the Presbyterian world, and permitted reading even on Sundays, along with missionary books now entirely forgotten). The iron kettle would be singing as it hung from its hook over the kitchen fire, the clock ticking on the wall, a white cloth spread on the table for our tea, a loaf from our weekly batch, butter from one or other of the neighbouring farms marked in the pretty lozenge-shaped pattern traditional in the neighbourhood, our own raspberry jam, in a ruby glass jam-dish; my glass of milk set aside from the morning on the cold slab of the larder, its cream a band at the top, narrower

44

or wider as the cow was newly calved or going dry. After tea, on the big rag hearthrug by the kitchen range, glossy with black lead, its steel dampers spotless and shining, Aunty Peggy would sit in the rocking-chair, taking from under its cushion (the place where newspapers and catalogues of all kinds were kept) the *Northern Presbyter* or the *Newcastle Daily Journal*; and I in the windsor chair, my feet on the steel fender, its lustre soft with much polishing, embroidering some afternoon-tea apron (those eighteenth-century garments were still worn on Sundays by the ladies of Bavington), handkerchief-sachet, or table-centre; french knots, feather-stitch, cross-stitch, faggoting, chain-stitch, satin-stitch, button-hole stitch, hem-stitch, whipping and smocking; I name them all, so far have those once familiar occupations of childhood's evenings—those satin-stitch violets and wild-roses, once in my eyes so beautiful, or that cross-stitched cats' tea-party I once embroidered on a tray cloth for my mother's brithday—receded into a past as remote as that of the Mithraic carvings and hypocausts of Housteads a few miles away. No more than the stonecutters on the Roman wall did I know as I embroidered, in cursive chain-stitched 'B.S.' (Bavington School) on the roller-towels for the school lobby, or laboriously copied 'A whistdrive and social will be held . . .' in copperplate script with those heavy down-strokes and fine up-strokes which I never mastered, that I was anonymously signing the imprint of a period.

These were the evening tasks, the evening pleasures, accepted as both task and pleasure; and because so accepted, the tasks and the days ('six days shalt thou labour and do all that thou hast to do') built round my childhood then a shelter of reality I have never since known: all was as it must be, could not be otherwise than be, secure and familiar.

But at bed-time the immeasurable forces of the dark were waiting beyond the kitchen door to seize upon me, to dissolve me into nothing, snatch me away from the small charmed circle of safety cast by the light. To leave the lamp-lit kitchen, to carry my enamel candle-stick with its precarious flame up the stairs to my cold bedroom with its blue wallpaper overgrown with patches of damp, each with a life of its own, in daylight like a plant of moss or lichen, but at night like some conscious presence, was to venture unprotected into the region of unknown powers. Safe I was if I looked at the candle-flame; but on the wide landing where along the book-shelves a fox's mask looked down and many closed doors led into rooms full of darkness, what lurked in the shadow that moved with me and behind me? Children sense how precariously the phenomenal world is held together, how thin the texture of its appearances, how easily torn to let in nothingness.

I was advised to say the Lord's Prayer when I was afraid; but the presence of God everywhere seemed then not the least terrifying aspect of the Great Mystery; and in terror I implored the Holy Ghost not to appear to me, in tongues of flame and with a sound like a rushing wind. Yet living as I did in the manse, with the stone kirk in our own garden and field, I had the sense of personal involvement with the things of God, feeding my imagination with those two books most accessible in all Bibles to the very young, Genesis and Revelation. On Sundays a fire was lit in the parlour where the piano stood, and the fragile porcelain vases with dried grasses, and I would read, too fearful to look up from the page, of the Apocalypse. During the first World War, Armageddon and the unsealing of the Seven Seals of the Book of Judgement seemed, to country people for whom the Bible was the true Word of God with the same literalness as the news in the *Newcastle Daily Journal*, the simple history of the near future. The advent of those crowned grasshoppers with the hair of women and the teeth of lions, the stars falling from Heaven and the moon turning to blood were events daily to be expected, though none knew when. Perhaps after all they were more right than subtler symbolists; I did not doubt that I should be among those present at the End of the World. Frightening as they might be, and strange beyond the power of invention, my imagination recognized in those dread visions an aspect of its own world.

The harsh Calvinism of the Presbyterian Kirk (my mother had suffered from Sabbaths behind drawn blinds, allowed to read only, besides the Bible, Fox's terrible *Book of Protestant Martyrs*) I never experienced; my terrors of the darkness had certainly nothing to do with the God of Calvin and Knox (such was then my innocence that it never occurred to me that I might be one of the wicked for whom Hell burned) but were archaic and instinctive; whatever it was I feared was not Hell, or punishment. That fierce morality was not the only aspect of the Old Testament which spoke to the Scottish temperament, after all: there was also the nature-poetry of Job and the Psalms, all of storm and wind and mountains and the deep, peculiarly suited to the landscape of Scotland, and to the way such children as myself responded to an untamed land. As for the Sabbath, my own memories have fashioned that day in an atmosphere of staid yet delicate sweetness.

On Sundays the heavy door of the little eighteenth-century stone church, locked at all other times, was opened for the one service—morning or afternoon on alternate Sundays—for which the Minister bicycled from Stamford-ham to our outlying congregation. Farmers and their tall Northumbrian wives came in traps, and the church stable was opened for their horses. The Minister and one or two of the farmers and their wives would stay to a sweet solemn Sunday dinner with us, in the dining-room never used but for guests; for since we lived in the manse, some of its dignities and its duties devolved upon us. The pasties, apple, rhubarb, gooseberry or raspberry (successors of those which so sumptuously furnished the house-warming) were made by myself, under my aunt's stern step-by-step supervision; they were always undersweetened—it was wartime, and this may have been a reason, but not the only reason: undersweetening, like the convention which permitted the sucking of acid-drops but no other sweet during the long sermon, had a moral, or perhaps it would be truer to say, an aesthetic value, impossible to define but impossible not to sense; austerity, plainness, is always most admirable when it is a matter of style rather than of principle, and our under-sweetened pasties partook in that subtle beauty of living signified by the grey Quaker gown, the Rule of St. Benedict or the Pythagorean abstinence from beans; abstinence from alcohol was a matter of moral principle, and therefore without that finesse which belongs only to manners, not to morals.

The front porch of the manse was opened on that day alone, a door of sacred dignity; no part of our lives on the six days of doing all that we had to do. There hung the Minister's black cassock; the Cromwellian Communion-cups and the tall slender church vases of green glass rimmed with gold were locked away in a cupboard of varnished pine. To find flowers for the church vases was my Sunday morning task; and in my pale blue wool-backed satin dress, embroidered with violets, my hair brushed loose, and scissors in my hand, I walked the garden-paths to cut suitable flowers; godly flowers.

To know godly from ungodly flowers is a part of my Presbyterian education that has remained with me; an instinctive sense of their intrinsic natures and symbolic, 'signatures'. Tall white pheasant's-eye narcissi; daffodils white or pale (but not the double yellow sort that grew in great clumps along the border of the vegetable-garden), white phlox (though with some reservations on account of its strong scent, distracting from devotion), and a certain white mallow were permitted. Madonna lilies, by their very name, were suspect, as idolatrous; the rose, the flower of love, was not encouraged; and once I was seriously scolded for bringing crimson peonies (too riotously loose-petalled,

48

and to the rose as profane is to sacred love) while to put tiger-lilies in the church vases I did not need Blake's Tyger to remind me was unthinkable. Not only was a combination (a 'clash' not a harmony) of black and orange manifestly ungodly, but the form of the flowers, with the tense recurve of the petals, the long filaments, too delicately extended, and hung with their heavily loaded anthers, spoke of nature's unconsecrated mysteries. There was something in so intricately perfect a form, besides, to arouse the intelligence, and by so doing to ruffle the surface of the glassy sea of calm devotion. Poppies verged on wickedness even as a garden flower. A pale yellow species of asphodel, long ago planted in the manse garden by a minister who had some knowledge of rare flowers, I myself spared; for I had a secret understanding with the asphodel, as a plant sacred to the Greek gods; its alien evanescent form, like its alien evanescent name, made it a flower apart, like the white Grass of Parnassus that grew high on our northern moors in certain wet places, but which participated in the nature of all that the name Parnassus signified. All wild flowers were, of course, altogether ungodly; to be 'wild' was, by definition, to be outside the Lord's Sabbath.

Yet I loved those Sundays, days kept as holy, wherein laborious people did no manner of work, and exchanged their week-day character and dress for something unaccustomed, dignified and refined by a grave sweet light shed about them by the archaic Word of God from the Holy Book. By those words, and those stories, so alien yet so familiar, we were all drawn away from ourselves into other selves with modes of thought and feeling unfamiliar and unpractised. Those unpractised other selves of simple people were like their polished parlours, with piano or the more holy harmonium none had skill to play, the family Bible, photographs of their ceremonially robed bridal selves, and of their dead, including the newly dead young soldiers killed in the war, enlarged from some stiff snapshot, as strangely unlike their homely selves as the sons of the wife of Usher's Well whose hats were of the birk; theirs the trench-caps of the British Army. These rooms were kept with reverence like a shrine, opened only upon the Sabbath Day, or for christenings, marriages, and funerals; those so deeply spiritual, and also so deeply carnal moments when life seemed raised into a higher and more solemn mode, struggling out of itself towards something which could be sensed but not described. In those ceremonial rooms exotic flowers bloomed with marvellous abundance: Christmas-cactus, maiden-hair and pheasant ferns, pendant white campanula, pelargoniums, treasured for their beauty as works of art in high social spheres, but even more for their rarity, or because grown from a cutting from the greenhouse of some Trevelyan or Shafto; plants of unknown name, valued for their strangeness as if perhaps there were no other on earth, like that Chinese orange tree which grows only in the Emperor's garden, or the small bindweed on Eriskay, planted by Prince Charles Edward Stuart which they tell you there is none like elsewhere in the world; so great in all human-kind is the desire to possess one treasure beyond all price and peerless. These scarcely literate country people did not live always and only in the profane; they felt, however remotely, the upward pull of simple and time-honoured observances through which they felt themselves securely bound within an order of values dimly and remotely glimpsed; as it were at the foot of Jacob's Ladder leading into that heaven whose glory, on holy days, unveiled itself a little. And it is perhaps those at the foot of the ladder who best can see its height.

In the evening when Aunty Peggy and I were left again in sole possession of the manse and the kirk, I was allowed to play on the church harmonium tunes from the hymn-book with its India-paper leaves, thin and holy, with their oval breves and semibreves. The engraved script of music seemed to me extremely beautiful, like an unknown sacred language, Sanskrit or Tibetan, a high language known to the angels themselves who to the sound of harps and trumpets sing hymns continually; a language I could divine but not decipher, full of intelligible meaning as yet unknown to me, speaking of a world remote from Bavington. The harmonium's strange voices, vox Humana, vox Angelica and Diapason (a name, to me, conferred on the thing named the nature implicit in the name) its windy petals, its groans, the stiff rattle of the damp keys, and my own child's voice singing holy words, exalted me into a Sunday rapture. 'They shall rise on wings, as eagles,' the Minister had read from the Holy Book, 'they shall run and not weary, they shall walk and not faint.' The eagle-wings were for youth, he had told us, as we sat, stiff and still in the varnished pews; the running for grown men, the walking for the old. Mr. Howatson was old; but I was young, never would I run or walk, but would rise always on wings, always and only soar.

And all the time it was growing darker and darker until the shadow invaded the holy sanctuary itself. Over the varnished pitch-pine of the pulpit a brass lamp twinkled faintly from the failing light outside. The red carpet led between empty pews (were they empty?) to the dark porch; and there, I knew, lurked evil-ones mustered against the holy as negative electricity is attracted towards positive. The more angels were gathered in the dim sanctuary of the church, the more demons thronged against them in the outer darkness, always in equal strength; for the outer darkness is their kingdom, boundless, immeasurable; and the angels (of course) could not leave the church, where they belonged. My heart thudding and my tongue cleaving to the roof of my mouth with terror so that I could not utter a prayer, I made my way between those empty pews, plunged into the gathering night, and along the church wall where lady's-mantle grew rank among coarse grass. Never have I known panic fear like that which possessed me as I fled along the side of the kirk, across the field into the

51

manse garden and up the path past the yew-trees that led to the door of the back-kitchen, behind the little wall overhung with ivy-leaved toad flax; lifting the latch I plunged into the darkness among the drums of paraffin, storm lanterns, buckets, the wooden washing-tub, the hip-bath, the wave of terror mounting behind me as the sneck of the kitchen door delayed my rush for safety. There the wave that had swept me in its course would break and those powers of immeasurable evil ebb into the ocean of outer darkness, as I reached the safety of the lamplight, my Aunty Peggy's human presence, and the table laid ready for the breakfast of a morning not holy: the sabbath, with its heights and depths of the numinous, was over.

I had at Bavington my first bosom friend, Sally Walton, one of the daughters of the farm of Throckrington. She was a year older than I and she seemed to me, with her dark brown hair, her rosy cheeks and her vivid red lips, altogether beautiful. Her voice was a rich contralto, with a kind of break in it, indescribable as voices are. She was strong and gay and she knew everything about animals and birds, about hay, and all the world of barn and byre to whose fringes I so precariously clung. Sally and her two younger sisters sometimes came to school on horseback, sometimes on foot, and in the evenings I would go with Sally half way home, or all the way. Through the farmyard; along a length of stone dyke; then through a gate onto a wilder pasture, with a ferny crag; to the Onsteads farm, and past a plantation of wind-scaped beeches. From there we could see Throckrington Church, and were on the land of Sally's own farm. There was a pool where a grebe nested, and once Sally showed me the nest and its clutch of wild eggs. On the way we asked one another riddles as old as the hills (where did we learn them? Why can I no longer remember them?) and told stories about 'an Englishman, an Irishman, and a Scotsman' which seemed to us inexhaustibly funny. There was no irony, no cynicism in our laughter; it was as classical as the jokes in Aristophanes and much less sophisticated. At Throckrington we would catch wild litters of kittens in the hay-loft where the swallows built in the high rafters, or seek eggs, or I would watch Sally while she milked with her skilful fingers. For her day's work began when she returned home. Her father was said to be immensely rich; but in those days farmers' sons and daughters worked on the farm, becoming farmers and farmers' wives in their turn, their knowledge passed on from father to son and mother to daughter—the best recipes for jam and cakes and the skills of baking all the loaves and pasties and rabbit pies that sustained their labour.

Why did I love Sally? Why she rather than her sister Molly, nearer my own age? Why did I despise Mrs. Carr's freckled granddaughter Hetty Thorburn, who lived much nearer to me than Sally? Who knows the answer to a question no child ever asks, love being so simple, so spontaneous when one is a child. Sally was my 'best friend' beyond all doubt or question. It was not that we had 'tastes in common'—though we had a world in common. Such relationships are a blessed gift of nature while we are still within our own nature.

It was many years later that I met Sally again; she had a handsome son of twenty-one, and a daughter called Kathleen. So it would seem that that thin-legged far away Kathie had remained a part of her life, even as Sally of mine; though now we must meet as strangers. Could we ever have believed it? In the grown-up world others might grow estranged, might go away to far-off places and never return; but we never would, for Bavington was the place of our happiness, and never would we go into the far world among strangers. Sally, married to a farmer, moved only a few miles; her sister Bella, married, lives now at Clay Walls; while I—can never return.

And yet it was not on the merry walk to Throckrington

with Sally and Molly and Bella, but on the walk back alone that I was most companioned, was nearest to the being of beings I loved: nature itself. I was an 'only child' and my solitude never seemed strange to me, or lacking anything heart could desire. Stories about the Englishman the Irishman and the Scotsman were one thing; but that was all a world of play and make-believe. Alone, the wind blew through my hair and through my heart, and every stone, every stonechat, every flower of eyebright or thyme, the polypody fern, the clouds far out over the moors, were as if part of myself. To be with other people, even with my best friend, was to be diminished to the stature of a little girl with mouse-coloured plaits and a velvet bandeau. Alone, I was all the earth, as far as the horizon and to the depths of the sky. Lacking nothing, desiring nothing but to be for ever in that place of all the earth that was mine, I knew—I think I am not inventing this in retrospect—perfect happiness. I knew that I was where I alone desired to be. It was by no will of mine that time moved on, and tore me from my early and humble roots.

Yet if I must tell all, I must tell of an episode which I can never forget, in which I was, God knows, the victim not the guilty, though it was I who killed. My dear grey tabby-cat, Graysie, a gift from Sally from the Throckrington barns, tolerated but not welcomed in the manse by Aunty Peggy, was the being I most loved at that time; for what child can ever love a human being with that osmosis of understanding with which we are at one with the animals? Animals never speak, and therefore never accuse, never blame us, always accept us just as we are. Graysie was my cat utterly; and when, though supposed a Tom, she proved a she, I remember how her striped body grew pear-shaped, and how I could feel the kick of the kittens inside her when I stroked her lazy pregnant side. And there one morning, in the box I had prepared for them, were the kittens, a warm snuggling pile. I was prepared to love them too, all of them. But my

Aunty Peggy not so: it was my cat, it was my responsibility that these unwanted kittens had been born; and it was I who must drown them.

Country people are cruel and realistic; my Aunty Peggy saw nothing more in this command than in an order to fill the water-crocks or to fetch the milk. So I must fill the zinc bucket, and I must drop in the kittens. They were asleep, they were quiet as I dropped them in; so quiet that I hoped death would not waken them. But they came alive, they struggled for life, I heard their tiny claws scratching the zinc. I trembled, my knees grew weak, I fled. Yet it was I who was made to dig their grave, to empty the contents of the bucket into the hole, to fill the hole in. That was the price of having a cat, and it was I who must take the consequences; I must 'learn my lesson', Aunty Peggy said. And all this I did. So young, blood was already on my hands.

My friend Sally perhaps would have thought little of drowning a litter of kittens; I do not know. Farms are places where birth and death are everyday events and no guilt attaches to murder. But it was not so with me.

It was winter, and I had caught a feverish chill through staying out in the icy wind for many hours, high up on the moor away from the houses, because Grannie Carr's pig was to be killed that day; my friend, to whom I had given bunches of elderberries and cabbage-leaves, visiting him in his stye, sometimes letting him loose in his field and there playing with him. So on that day I ran away far enough, as I hoped, not to hear his shriek. I was not sure whether or not I heard it, after all; in imagination I did, and yet still listened; the wind itself seemed to carry his death on it. All was long over when at last I returned; I had walked on the thin ice of a cattle's drinking-trough, and going in up to the knees my clogs and stockings were soaked with cold water. Knowing that I would be scolded for getting my feet wet, I lingered in the steel-like wind hoping it would dry me. My teeth were chattering with cold when at last I was undressed by the kitchen fire and my feet restored to life in a footbath of mustard-and-water. There were no hot-water bottles in those days; or if there were, not in the manse; and in the always-damp feather-bed I first shivered and then burned. Next day I had a fever, and a fire was lit in my blue bedroom; and lying in bed I watched the flames and glowing palaces; a fire in a bedroom was a luxury which made illness a pleasure. But I remember watching as I lay the shifting and writhing patterns of ribbons and roses, and the patches of damp on the blue wallpaper, and the waxing and waning of the substantiality of the room, upon whose reality I could keep no hold. Neither the Fifth Commandment in its gilt frame, with painted angels blowing their trumpets among calligraphic scrolls of red and blue and green; nor the wool sampler, *I am the True Vine*, cling to them as I might as icons of the holy and secure, could hold my world together.

I do not remember the way of transition from that feverish room into the freedom of the clear dark sky in which I found myself travelling accompanied by a dark winged companion, a sort of bird-angel or *alter ego* whose features I could not see and did not try to see. We were rising swiftly and beautifully through the night, and I knew the destination, towards which I travelled as a place I had always known. There was a sense of perfect familiarity, as of something formerly known and now remembered. We were travelling, as I thought, to some star; but I cannot be certain for we never reached that place, and the pull of the earth began to draw me back; alone now. Presently I saw the bedroom, as another kind of space, another world coming into place. I remember how small the window with its sixteen panes looked, as I came back into my body to find my mother putting water into my mouth from a tea-spoon.

Yet I came back willingly enough; indeed, as it seemed to me, of my own accord; for I was happy on earth, then, and loved no place on earth as I loved the manse, and its garden, and its moors and the horizon bounded by the three humps of Simonside. I came back as gladly as that other Cathie whom Emily Brontë describes weeping, in a dream, until the angels should carry her back to earth and put her down at Wuthering Heights. Like a wild animal I loved my wild lair; and to return from my night-journey of the soul to the manse, the moors, the crags, the burn running at the foot of the garden under the blackcurrant bushes and the mounds of saxifrage, to the raspberry canes under the high stone wall overgrown with its mosses of many beautiful forms, the liver-wort on the outcrop of rock by the out-houses, the scent of the cream-flowered daphne on the thaw-fragrant winter air, seemed not a grief but a delight. Even so, I knew on my return that there had been a closing, a limiting, a diminution as the world slipped into place. That leaving of the body was for a state not tenuous and fragmentary or dreamlike, but more clear, more real than normal consciousness in this present world. As into this world we wake from sleep, so into that we wake from waking.

Of my excursion out of the body I did not at the time, or for half a life-time after, think as perhaps a foresight of the road all travel at death; and I continued to regard death with the same grief and horror that drove me away onto the icy moor when the pig was slaughtered. The violent parting of soul from body, commonplace as it is to every country child, the instinctive energy of life refuses to accept. How much does the pity and terror of tragedy itself rest upon this bodily *timor mortis*? Traditional wisdom, whether of Vedanta or the Buddhist scriptures, of the vision of Dante or Blake, precludes tragedy; for the possibility of the hells (whether of finite or of infinite duration), is not the same thing as Aristotle's 'pity and terror', which is of this world, and at its centre such a death as we share with the animals we slaughter.

Over the high moss-grown stone wall of the manse

garden, behind the raspberry canes where on hot summer days I basked and read the novels of Sir Walter Scott on the wooden bench of a little holly-arbour, was the bull-field. There the bull lived his solitary life, marked out from the herd by the brass ring in his nose, and the heavy wrinkled folds of his head and neck. We children used often to play a dangerous game of 'last across' the bull-field, climbing the five-barred gate from the farmyard when he was quietly grazing at the far end of his field; or we would provoke him with sticks, poked with safety over the wall, to make him advance with lowered head, that ominous slowness gathering to a rush that filled us with delight and terror. His high-pitched bellow was well known to me, for from my bedroom window I could see into his field when the other children had gone home to their distant farms—in a special sense he was my neighbour.

Anyone who has lived on, or by, a farm, knows in what respect a bull is held. There is no other creature on an English farm who has the power of death in his horns. For this reason, and also no doubt because of his sexual potency, equated with 'sin', he was the evil-one of our world. Yet by us children the bull's *mana*, his magical animal power, was recognized; he was a power among us; no human being in our world had such greatness as his. Theriomorphic gods are older than human, and children, like archaic man, recognize with immediacy the quality of animal-souls. He was, besides, not *a* bull, but *the* bull. Like the priest of the sacred wood, there is never more than one.

One day—I think in March, but this is no more than an impression of a clear cold sparse day of early spring—the news passed round among us that the bull had gored the farmer; not fatally, as it happened, for his eldest son, a boy of thirteen, and still one of the back row of pupils in my Aunt's school-room, had arrived on the scene in time to save his father's life. But the butcher had been sent for, and the bull was to die.

So it was that I was one of the row of children who stood in the farmyard, where on an outcrop of rock the camomile was trodden by the clogs and hooves of all the village; the same farmyard where daily I filled our two buckets from the well. The farmyard was our Akropolis; and there we gathered to witness an event that held us not in partial, but in total, all-excluding participation. Never in amphitheatre nor temple of the gods nor circle of stone menhirs did the fate of consecrated victim more totally absorb the minds and souls of the spectators; what the theatre only represents, the bull-fight simulates, this was.

I recall the hush as the butcher drove his low dray into the farmyard; it stood there, empty, while the butcher walked over to the byre; empty; but we know what it was— a hearse for the dead. And the great one who was to be dead still lived, not knowing he was to die. The human world had passed judgement on the animal; the evil beast must yet again be slaughtered. Behind the immediate crime—the attack upon man—lay who knows what remote echo of archaic man's profound self-condemnation of his own animal nature, still not extinct in men so primitive as to be scarcely themselves securely rooted in the human principle to which on the Sabbath Day they aspired. Unreflectingly these hamlet-dwellers passed on the beast the age-old human verdict, laid down for the animal in the antiquity of pre-history; yet for them there was drama in his death as though the struggle between man and animal remained still undecided, still to be waged. There was in this death the suspense of a struggle undecided: why else did we gather and stand so attentively on our limestone akropolis?

But to me the pity was greater than the terror: I was on his side. Everyone knew, as I did, that Farmer Bell was but a poor specimen of mankind; his stone dykes were falling unmended, his children were dirty and covered with ringworm, his wife a slattern and he himself was good for nothing but breeding his kind; yet now all but I sided with him against the innocence of nature. Such was human solidarity; but I was on the side of nature against man; I felt the wrong man was committing against the wildness of the beast, who, having no conscience had not sinned. Surely, surely he must not die! Justice would intervene, what justice I did not know, but I believed the world to be just.

There was the long waiting; the butcher, alone, crossing the yard, gun in hand; a muffled bellow; and as in a Greek tragedy the king is slain behind the heavy doors of his palace, so we waited for the shot, and knew that the great one of our small world, the creature of power, had once again been slaughtered; the strong by the weak, the great by the small. Presently, as from those palace doors, the great body was dragged out of the byre and onto the dray, limp and powerless. I saw his pepper-and-salt purplish-brown hide with a sense of infinite compassion: I *was* him. My body suffered in itself the death of the beast, my skin mourning for his skin, my veins for his veins, my five senses for his; and when from his anus slipped a mass of faeces, I was ashamed for the abasement of his death.

In another death my participation was of a darker kind. I had a boy-cousin, a year younger than myself, with whom I had often played as a child; he must, when his sudden death put an end to his childhood, and, as it seems, to my own, have been eleven years old, I twelve. It was Easter, and I, with my parents, was at the manse; not any more living there, but already moving away into an exile from which I was never to return. I was a visitor to what had once seemed my own place. We had scarcely, as it seems, arrived, when a telegram came to say that my cousin was dead. My father, I remember, knelt down and prayed on the stone flags of the manse kitchen floor, my Aunty Peggy weeping loudly, and I myself strangely embarrassed by my father's act, which seemed so out of keeping with the familiar manse kitchen; and by my Aunty Peggy's loud weeping, strangely out of character. Then we all left for the Midland town where his parents then lived, to attend the funeral. I think I was more sorry to leave Bavington than that Jimmy was dead.

He had been, on Easter day, to the Presbyterian church; and on the way home (his parents had stayed on for the Communion service) had said to another boy with whom he was walking, 'It is so dark and cold on this side of the road, let us cross into the sun.' Then he had collapsed and had never recovered consciousness, dying two days later of cerebral meningitis. I did not see him dead; dared not, would not go to look at him; but his death invaded and possessed me.

The horror that took possession of me was, literally, a darkening of the light. The light was filled with blackness, the light itself was emptied of light; not figuratively, but in a way those only who have known the like will understand, the phenomenal world ceased to be accessible to me. For me the bright Easter sun was dark, shedding blackness. I could see objects about me, and people, but I could not reach them; they and I were in the same physical space, but between them and me there was a great gulf fixed. Was I possessed by my cousin's young and too suddenly banished spirit, whose last conscious act was to seek the light? Was what I then suffered not my own, but an invasion of what he was suffering in the darkness of his sudden death, unable either to reach the people or the things of this world, or to make his way elsewhere? Are our spirits in truth so separate that such influx and possession by the thoughts of others may not occur? It was as if I as well as he had died from the living world and that bright Easter sunlight.

No one had any idea of what I was suffering, for who has words to describe those states that absolutely remove the normal aspect of the visible and tangible world from the reach of consciousness? I was in terror, even in broad daylight, of being alone, lest the gulfs of darkness should swallow me.

My mother must have stayed to comfort her sister; for I

remember going on, with my father, to stay with his two second cousins, Marie and Sally, at the little village post office in County Durham, and the blackness went with me. I remember looking at brilliant golden dandelions in the sun, and their being entirely filled with blackness, emptied of all substantial reality. I clung to my father's hand as if only physical contact with his calm life, as he walked with God, could hold me to this world.

What I suffered was not grief; not mourning. I was sorry for my cousin's death but not as they grieve who lose one deeply loved. It was not even 'fear of death', but rather an invasion of consciousness by death, if so I may call the total removal of all contact with what we are accustomed to experience as a world. There are states of insanity in which the loss of reality is continuous; but to call such a condition insane is to evade the most obvious conclusion to be drawn from the experience as such: that the sensible world coheres not by physical but by mental agency. At best it coheres precariously; there is nothing inherently safe or solid about the sensible world, even though normally, at least by daylight, and in adult life, we accept it for real without giving the matter a thought. It is a marvel of adaptation that we do so.

Bavington seems, in retrospect, to have ended with that Easter. Perhaps it was in truth many years before I returned; or perhaps memory has now amended the pattern of the outer to fit the inner reality, which engulfed my own childhood in that annihilating darkness.

My father's people I scarcely knew; and the only house on his side of the family in which I remember having stayed was the little village post office at Newfield kept by Marie and Sally Pearson, his cousins; the house where the ferns and oxalis had made for themselves a sanctuary in the enclosed back yard. But I must have visited other houses; for from them I retain an impression (remote perhaps because I have put away from me such memories) of the crude raw stench of the poverty of the working-class. I remember the dirty miners' children who came into that little post office, very often sent by their mothers to ask for goods on credit; I can remember hearing Aunt Marie sending away a little girl, telling her, as it now seems to me, that her mother could have no more until she paid. The episode shocked me, though from what point of view I don't know; I think just the uncovering of unhappiness and anger and the sense of lives irremediably wrong. I remember that some of those children took me one day into a stifling kitchen, where a slatternly woman was frying onions. The strong smell overcame me and I held my nose. The woman laughed at me for this, and I was overcome with shame at having seemed impolite; I denied that it was the smell of her kitchen I minded.

Another impression is of a narrow and squalid brick yard in a pit-row, perhaps the house of one of my father's brothers. On the ground was the dirtiest crawling baby I had ever seen, her bottom and legs ingrained with dirt as she dragged herself about on the ground. The smell of the human animal nauseated me. And yet I have another memory, of walking hand in hand with a gentle bearded old man, my father's father. I was gathering sea-pinks on a shore, and he holding them for me; so the place must have been Newbiggin in Northumberland, where one of my mother's sisters had the infants' school.

It was natural that, coming from such a world, my father should look forward to a better future, and not back into a legendary past; yet his people too had lived their banishment within sight of the countryside from which their fathers had been driven by poverty from the fields to the pits. For my father lost Eden was not over the Border, but, no less inaccessible, in the pre-industrial England of Gainsborough and Surtees and Constable and Bewick that still survived between the pit-villages. These were the painters (as Cowper and Wordsworth the poets) my father most loved. I have seen him stand, lost in memory, contemplating some country lane or painted plough like the one he had learned to guide seventy-five years before. To him Constable's plough was a transcript of that real plough he had himself known the feel of in his hands, and the horses and the fields and the lanes and the cloudy skies not a world of imagination but reality itself, recaptured in a pictured world. For as a schoolboy he had played truant to drive the horses on a neighbouring farm, and at the end of his childhood wept when he was forced against his will, being a clever and docile boy, to become a pupil-teacher. At eighty-five his bitterest regret was that he had not been allowed to become a labourer in the fields of that lost paradise of the English countryside. His first love was a daughter of Sir William Eden's gamekeeper; and with the loss of that early love he lost, too, all hope of any return to a way of life and a world as a tiller of the fields from which his forefathers had been driven.

My father's lost Eden was the English countryside and English nature-poetry and landscape-painting spoke to him and for him; but from his boyhood his only cultural heritage was the Methodist Christianity his father had inherited from his grandfather who had walked, so my father would often tell us, twenty miles to hear John Wesley preach, and twenty miles back, to go down the pit on a Monday morning, strengthened in that darkness by his faith in another world than that cave where prisoners are chained. My old gentle grandfather was a class-leader among the Wesleyans, a man of blameless goodness; he had himself gone down the pit when he was eight years old, often not seeing the light of day from one Sunday to the next; yet I think he lived his life, enduring many sorrows (the loss of his wife when my father was himself eight years old and of a daughter who had barely reached eighteen when my father was at college) in the deep and abiding joy of an unshakeable faith; his favourite book, after the Bible, was Thomas à Kempis's *Imitation of Christ*. He also knew many healing herbs; centaury, agrimony, and other wild plants, hung in bunches to dry in his kitchen. With these he cured the simple ailments of his family in days when poor men could not afford to call a doctor unless in extreme need.

Yet quite unknown to himself my father was heir to a religion far different and of greater antiquity, from ancestors forgotten. But it was as a children's game, long emptied of *mana*, that he inherited the mystery of that old battle between the champions of light and darkness whose issue, however many times it be fought, remains always undecided. As a little boy in County Durham he had been initiated, unawares, into a tradition older than Christianity, surviving in the 'guiser's play', handed down by the older to the younger boys in secrecy and by word of mouth. In the week before Christmas—the winter solstice—the little boys, with faces blackened with soot and wearing their fathers' jackets turned inside-out by way of actors' costume, would go from house to house, knocking at the doors. First would enter 'King George',

> 'Here comes in King George,
> King George is my name,
> With sword and pistol by my side
> I hope to win the game.'

—then his enemy 'The Turkish Knight',

> 'The game sir? The game sir?
> That lies in my power!
> I'll cut you into mincemeat
> In less than half an hour.'

—and the King with the earth-name, the Green Knight and the black-faced enemy, would then fight until the enemy lay slain on the rag hearthrug before the kitchen fire. Then the victor himself, inexplicably and illogically changing his mood, would call for 'the Doctor' (my father usually played 'the Doctor') to come and revive the slain. 'Is there a doctor?' he says; and from the darkness outside a chorus of little boys answers,

'No doctor!'
'A pound for a doctor!'
'No doctor!'
'Five pounds for a doctor!'

Still no doctor; and the bidding would go on with mounting tension until a price was named that, after whispering and a pause outside, brought in the travelled and cloaked figure of 'Doctor Brown' ('Here come I, Old Doctor Brown, the best old doctor in the town') wearing an old top hat and carrying his famous bottle of the elixir of life. The doctor is asked to tell how he came by his knowledge; and his answer goes back to the late middle-ages when Paracelsus and his like travelled

'Italy, Picardy, France and Spain
Round the world and back again.'

The Turkish knight, magically revived, would spring to his feet, and the champions, reconciled, would make a promise (not to be broken until the next solstice) 'we'll never fight no more'. The guisers still outside in the cold would then come thronging in for their share of the oranges or ginger-cordial now distributed to all. That was the Christmas play; no one thought of asking why there was no Christianity in it.

Driven underground, did an old paganism unrefined by song and poetry linger on in the imagination of the tillers of the soil of Durham and Yorkshire, unsubdued by that newer religion whose excessive insistence upon the virtues of meekness and love was perhaps the measure of the brutality of that which it was invoked to subdue? Typical of many similar stories (murder and the gallows in nearly all)

66

was one my father told of a farmer who in his loft kept an ox-hide with horns and tail complete. On a fine evening he would sometimes put on this theriomorphic disguise, lurk behind hedges and frighten his neighbours in whose souls, as in his own, albeit unknown to themselves, the horned god still reigned. In this story there is no mention of a coven; though it now seems to me more than likely that the farmer of the story was the 'devil' of a coven. In any case, the half-animal figure of the Devil still had power over the imagination of many a respectable church-goer for whom his hoofs and horns were an article of Christian faith.

A young hired man had recently come to the farm, and had been sent to the village forge with the coulter of a plough to be sharpened for the spring ploughing. The farmer felt the urge, so my father's story went, to put on his ox-guise and to enjoy, together with the sense of power to be had from frightening his neighbours, who knows what exaltation in his temporary identification with the archaic animal mood he donned with the skin of the beast with whom his life was so closely bound up in the fields he shared with his cattle. Hiding behind a hedge he appeared suddenly with a bellow that had made others take to their heels; but the lad, coulter in hand, stood his ground and faced this apparition of the evil-one. The boy, between terror and religious fervour, attacked with the coulter, and killed the devil; but it was the farmer whose blood soaked the fields fertilized in a forgotten past, it may be, with many blood-sacrifices made to the same god who had returned unrecognized to possess the human victims of that crudely enacted tragedy.

In a story so expressive of the mode of consciousness in that dim half-awareness of ignorance and animality, I seemed to catch a glimpse, beyond the fervour of my father's religion of love and goodness, of a dark ancestral contrary, brutal and heavy; a chthonic barbarity in every

67

way alien to my mother's world. The modes of feeling expressed by the songs of Scotland are delicate in their subtleties of tenderness, pride, scorn, nostalgia or mourning or merriment; and the 'other' world of Scotland is peopled with green-clad fairies of more than human beauty, or the bird-souls of the dead, or the terrible grandeur of the banshee not with the half-animal devil and churchyard ghosts; an elegant world.

The drama of my father's people was all a confrontation of good and evil in their crudest terms; men and women were either good and religious chapel-goers, or violent, drunken and brutal; or so it always seemed from the stories he told, many of which were of those spectacular 'conversions' so dear to the Methodists. My father never tired of describing these, and the revival meetings at which such conversions often took place. There he had himself seen and heard, as a boy, converted men 'speaking with tongues', or walking, in ecstatic trance, along the inch-wide tops of the chapel pews. To him such things seemed marvels of God. The crucial question was, in that world, 'salvation', and salvation meant some dramatic 'change of heart', a change of consciousness closely allied to mass emotion. But I found the 'salvation' of my father's world as remote as the state of the reprobate; his terms were, and have remained, alien to me.

These issues, among my mother's people, who were at once more naïve and more refined than those ardent aspirants towards salvation, simply never arose. Perhaps Calvin's doctrine of predestination precludes for those who hold it the Wesleys' wrestlings with the Traveller Unknown or John Bunyan's heart-searchings; the question of salvation or damnation rests with the Lord, and therefore there is, within that rigid doctrine, some room for freedom from the burden of personal guilt. I always had the impression, with members of my mother's family, that their religion was extraneous to themselves whereas the songs and history and fairy-lore of Scotland expressed their true natures and real beliefs. To escape into that world of poetry whose people have no morality but only life and its many moods must have seemed for them—and was for me—like an escape into reality from the acting of a tedious part; when moral censure was passed—as it often was—it might be vehement but it was never, I felt, sincere. To my father it was the other way: songs and stories and poetry he felt to be lacking in seriousness unless they had a moral; but what is the moral of the stories of Wallace or the Four Marys? The tears they brought were for beauty and valour, not of repentance and 'conviction of sin'. My mother's family put on their religion on Sunday with their Sunday clothes (which mattered to them no less, indeed perhaps much more, than religion) and during the rest of the week gave a degree of attention to this world which to my father seemed profane. My grandmother, grim slave of housework as she was (on her washing-days she generated an atmosphere of bitter and self-righteous resentment), had a certain fine fastidiousness; she would drink her tea only from the thinnest of china cups and these of gleaming cleanness; and she stirred her cream into Melrose's tea with a silver teaspoon.

My grandfather's three passions were likewise incomprehensible to my father, for none had any moral purpose; his fuchsias and gloxinias, the nemophila and the pansies, the sweet-peas and the gladioli he grew with a finesse which in my father's eye mere flowers could never deserve. When he was dying it was to look at his flowers that he came downstairs for a last time. My grandfather's second skill was dry-fly fishing; many a salmon he drew from the Tyne, and he himself made those delicate feather flies bound in the barbed hooks of which he always carried a few in his tweed cap. I loved to sit near him on the bank of the Tyne while he drew in on his line trout whose fragrance, in his fishing-creel so elegantly constructed of fine wicker, was like violets.

On account of his third passion—whisky—he was placed, by my father, unquestionably (though with regret, on my mother's account) among the wicked. This judgement was self-evident, and was that of his wife and daughters also. To 'drink' was sinful, sin was to 'drink'; so it was in that time, and place, and class. Such too was the teaching of the Kirk, whose moral condemnation was reserved for acts easy to discern in others, easy to avoid by the righteous. The subtleties of Dante's morality were as undreamed-of as those of the psychology of the unconscious, which has since made such havoc of these simple moral judgements. It is true that my grandfather's addiction to whisky had brought him down in the world; the hamlet of Kielder, remote from any source of supply, was the bottom of the descent. But why my brilliant and handsome grandfather had taken to drink, none asked. What my own generation would regard as effect was then regarded as cause.

Even my mother, whose real self was light-hearted, amoral and gentle had a second personality, the censorious Calvinist group-mind of the family collective, the terrible possessing devil of John Knox's Scotland. Censoriousness would come upon her, not, so far as I remember, in relation to people so much as in her relation to the inanimate world. If a weed grew in a flower-bed or a bush overhung the lawn, moral censure was invoked as if the weed were wicked and the bush deliberately doing wrong. Even chairs that stood in her way, or cups that got themselves broken, were blamed as agents—'that chair!'—whose perverse wills opposed and thwarted her. This sinister animism was, to be sure, the dark side of my mother's sense of the poetry of things; and she may after all have been right. Yet it was the inanimate world she turned her Calvinistic censoriousness upon. She had a particular voice, on such occasions, unlike her own, as if she were then possessed by a spirit of righteous indignation. When one or other of my 'aunties' came to stay, or when we were staying with my grandparents, this

70

collectivity would reabsorb my pretty mother into itself. I would lie in bed hearing the family voices rising and falling in censorious cadences something like the crooning voices of eider-duck, but loaded with an emotion of deep moral indignation. I used to think this censure was directed against me; for all the doctrine of the reprobate was expressed in those voices whose words I could not distinguish but whose rise and fall carried condemnation until my heart beat with dread. In adolescence 'the unforgivable sin' became a terror; for none could tell me what that sin was. Might I not commit it unawares? Had I not indeed already committed it? For the sense of guilt that had been implanted in me from earliest childhood by those accusing voices, before I knew what sin was. I feared with vital dread that to commit the unforgivable sin might be my fate.

For my mother the unforgivable sin was 'drink'; or rather it was so for her second self that belonged to her family collective. And I remember an episode very clearly in which I was the observer—from another state of being, like that calm virgin in Picasso's Tauromachia—of adult morality in action.

I must have been five or six at the time; which must have been during my father's summer holiday, which we spent always with my maternal grandparents. I was walking with my grandfather through fields to a neighbouring farm; he walking slowly, quietly puffing at his pipe; while I ran to and fro after white caps in the grass which I hoped would be mushrooms but which were very often only puff-balls. The late afternoon sun was golden on the dry sweet pasture with its eyebright and tormentil and wind-rustling harebells and quaking-grass. We were both happy to be free and away from the constrictions of the house, for my grandmother had had one of her washing days. We called at the farm; and I can clearly see, to this day, the farmer offering my grandfather a dram of whisky. In my mind's eye I can still see him standing by the sideboard draining the small glass of golden

71

liquid. Then we set off on our way home in the late summer gloaming and the shadows lengthening on the turf of that sweet pasture.

I remember nothing more until the outbreak of hatred that was suddenly shaking the house; and I was somehow in the centre of it: how could he have done such a thing and the innocent bit bairn with him? My poor grandfather at bay was allowed no word in his own defence by my grandmother, my aunts, my father, and even—to me unaccountably—by my own mother. It seemed that some great wrong had been committed, of which I was the innocent victim; but why, after that happy walk through the fields, I should have become the pretext of this ugly, devastating outburst of righteousness I could not understand. Indeed I did try to defend my grandfather; for I felt that I somehow shared his guilt, that I was the cause of this attack upon him. If he had done wrong so had I, for we had shared that walk which now appeared to have been such a dreadful thing. But I was snatched away to bed by my mother—excessively and demonstratively tender towards me—as the storm raged on. Children absorb such violent emotions by a kind of osmosis; and the sense remained with me that I was implicated in some terrible and mysterious sin. All the grown-ups had become ugly and dreadful, and now I could hear my grandfather turning on my mother, and knew not where my loyalties might lie.

My mother's one moral imperative—'never touch drink' —I could never hear without thinking of my grandfather set upon by the furies of his household; and it is abstainers rather than drunkards from whom I shrink to this day.

My father I think counted, also, my grandfather's striking good looks against him; or saw them perhaps rather as an extenuating circumstance, like a physical or mental defect; for physical beauty, whether in man or woman, constituted if not a sin, at least a predisposition to sin, a temptation

72

greater than is laid upon commoner and humbler clay. My mother and all her sisters were in their youth beautiful, with a kind of radiance that still shines from old photographs of them; a radiance later life extinguished in them all, though all kept their fine features, their curly abundant hair, and their slender lissom figures.

My mother's evasion, after her marriage, of the religion of John Wesley was not different from her earlier evasion of John Knox; a withdrawal of attention, a failure of interest availed her more than argument and useless opposition. She had, besides, a habit of fainting in church; I never knew her to faint elsewhere, certainly not at the theatre, on the longest walk, or in the hottest greenhouse in Kew. My father I think never knew whether my mother had been 'saved' or not; for she always agreed with everything he said. But at over eighty it was the Upanishads and the works of A. E. and G. R. S. Mead and even Israel Regardie that my mother would take down from my shelves, or travels in Tibet, or works on spiritualism; never have I seen her read any work of Christian devotion. The supernatural world was for her, as were her vivid nightly dreams, rather an escape from the moral world than, as for my father, a region of it. She confessed to me (she was in her mid-eighties then) that she was not 'religious' and had always found the emotionalism of Methodism vulgar; 'but I am very interested in the cosmos'. Some time before this she had had a slight stroke and thought she was dying. What was it like? I asked her; and my mother's eyes flashed like those of a hawk whose hood is lifted and she said 'I was very interested'.

And later still—in her nineties now, and after my father's death—my mother saw me with a little Victorian copy of Bunyan's *Pilgrim's Progress* given me by a friend to pass on to my grandchildren. 'I have never read it', she said; and I— missing her point—offered it to her. No, she said, 'I have avoided reading it all my life. But I know pretty well what is in it.' (This I can well believe, for to my father it was a

73

sacred book.) 'I think it is a book that has outlived its usefulness,' was my mother's last word. And then I read it myself.
She was more right than I—remembering how as a child I
had loved those chained lions, and the shepherds on the
Delectable Mountains with their glass through which Pilgrim saw the Holy City; how I had feared the thundering
mountain, and Apollyon, and that trap-door into Hell
through which the groans of burning sinners could be
heard—could have believed.

For did not the Bedford Tinker's Vanity Fair hold all the
glory of the Renaissance, stifled by the 'curse of Cromwell';
the theatre Shakespeare had created to civilize a nation;
Inigo Jones, and all the grace of seventeenth-century music?
Ignorance then as now seeks in bewildered envy to destroy
what it cannot possess; what it cannot even perceive—for if
it could see the beauty it would no longer be ignorance,
and no longer would wish to violate and destroy. Yet those
sour world-hating Puritans my father reverenced as saints
of his religion; those smashers of all the riches of English
Gothic sculpture, of the images of the Virgin, Refuge of
Sinners. To the Puritan to give refuge to sinners is indeed
the unforgivable sin of condoning sin. For what is worse in
Bunyan than his ignorant rejection of all culture as worldly
wickedness is the continual censure, the self-approving
condemnation of humanity as such. Those who had a 'conviction of sin' can only condemn their fellow-men and
women; seeing no beauty in the joyousness of Sir Toby
Belch and his night revels, in the innocence of the happy;
sick of self-love indeed, they only wish to see the poor
sinner brought, all his happiness turned to tears and bitter-
ness, to the stool of repentance. Of this taint of righteousness my father was not free; my mother, thank God, was;
she never thought herself good or made any effort to be so.
She had the gift of forgetting all the sin in the world in the
joy of watching some falling leaf or opening flower.

My father, on the contrary, was without curiosity because

74

for him all was settled long ago, when on the verge of manhood he himself underwent conversion to what he himself called—and indeed it was—'a living faith', a life-long orientation which needed no confirmation from books, from which indeed too much reading would have been only a distraction. Civilization with all its arts and expressions remained for him (as for those 'early Christians' the Roman slaves who were his models) beside the point. For my mother truth was imagination, was beauty, was nature. Yet a fineness of moral sense lent to my father's conduct a beauty of its own which to some might seem of a higher kind than that beauty 'blithesome and cumberless' worn by my grandfather's daughters as unthinkingly as birds wear their plumage.

Of, and into, this disparity I was born; my inheritance an irreconcilable conflict of values to which my parents dared never confess, or did not, perhaps, consciously recognize.

CHAPTER TWO

Is this the Region, this the Soil, the Clime,
Said then the lost Arch Angel, this the seat
That we must change for Heav'n ...

I AM writing, on this day in early November, in the gardens of Ninfa. I hear the sound of bird-song, and of gardeners at work with sickle and spade, and of the sweet bell of the church of Norma on the hill above. All this landscape has been inhabited by man, loved and tended by man, re-created by man, since the Cyclops lived behind the still solid walls of their village that crowned the crest before the Volscians gave their name to these hills terraced with olives; each tree, as in Greece, with its embankment of stones to keep the soil from washing away. A landscape made by man; in this garden bright with sinuous rills trout, of a species said to have been brought by Hannibal, swim in the clear waters, sacred to the nymphs when Pliny wrote of them. A pope was crowned in the church whose ruins now are entwined with rose and jasmin, and the slender leaves of grey mimosa move gently in the protection of its walls. In the Lombard tower is set a plate brought from Persia in the ninth century; others have fallen away leaving round discs in the tufa walls. In the apse of another church (it shelters a rock-garden now) the rain has not washed away nor the sun faded the contours of two madonnas, one of the eighth, the other of the eleventh century. The indelible line of intellectual beauty is still visible upon the crumbling plaster, as they recede in time while remaining still in place. On yet another wall, among persimmon trees, a fragment of a Nativity with Ox and Ass dates from the

76

century after St. Francis. Jackdaws live in the tower of the old castle, pink in the evening light like a back-cloth for one of Shakespeare's Italian plays. I think of Milton's Paradise; of Shelley writing his *Prometheus Unbound* in the baths of Caracalla; of a letter Edwin Muir wrote me (he too visited this garden, hospitable to poets) in which he spoke of the images everywhere of the Christian mysteries, of the Angel who greets the Virgin in the shrines men and women pass as they come and go in the streets of their ancient cities. Under my window-ledge the waters race; and here grows every tree that is pleasant to the sight, and good for food; orange, lemon, mandarin, avocado; magnolias, roses, cypress; fish-tanks of stone; parsley and violet. All is beautiful as that first garden tended by man; and beyond the avenue of walnut with trailing vines between, peach orchards, and beyond the orchards the fertile landscape of the Pontine marshes—drained by a former Duke of Sermoneta, uncle of my hostess. Even this newest change made by man upon the old landscape of Italy has beautified the scene. Between the rose-grown ruins of Ninfa, little changed since Edward Lear made drawings of this tower, and Circe's isle set in the glitter of the sea, there lie new fields and new villages, harmoniously green and fertile under the hillside where little flocks of sheep are still penned in the Cave of Polyphemus. A gardener is passing, carrying on his head a basket of little black grapes, the last of the season, to the house, formerly the hall of the mediaeval town of Ninfa. In that hall now the newest books in many languages lie on the table of the last Duchess, patron of literature from the world of Henry James, editor, before the last war, of *Commerce*, and after, of *Botteghe Oscure*, in whose pages the poets of England, France and America were published. On the piano on which Liszt performed, a sister-in-law of my host played, on the day after my arrival, Chopin's third Ballade; my hostess paints and plants this garden, which her mother and her grandmother created. All here reflects a beauty conceived by the human

77

imagination; and the servants in the house, the shepherds on the hill both young and old, the old women and the boys and girls in the steep streets of Sermoneta on its citadel, they too are graced with the dignity of Catholic Italy. Perhaps a generation from now this labour of ages will have gone; perhaps even sooner; for the tide of destruction is advancing, here as elsewhere. There are rumours of the waters of the nymphs being diverted for industrial development; and the civilization that here has been slowly matured and long guarded against barbarian invasion will be swept away.

With what reluctance I bring myself to look away from all this beauty (and for all it may be doomed, it is here and now still as I write), into those times and places of my own past of which I must now tell. Walking in this garden I have thought of the strangeness of the journey that has brought me by wanderings so devious, to the very heart of Italian civilization; the highest ever attained by western mankind. Soon I must leave again, travelling into the always inconceivable future; but once to have seen is to know for ever that such things are possible.

I have written of my years in Northumberland as if they had preceded in time all that belonged to other phases of my life; but that is not so. Northumberland was anterior only in a symbolic sense: not only because from beyond the Border came my ancestors, but also because there I found, in the few short years I lived at the manse with my Aunty Peggy Black, my own image of a Paradise already lost long before my birth. For I was not even born in Northumberland but in an East London suburb.

Yet all through my childhood, and for long after, it was Northumberland which seemed my home, enduring and real; and my father's house unreal, impermanent, a place not lived-in except for the time being. In part I may have reflected my mother's unspoken thoughts; but I believe it is also true that imagination accepts only what corres-

78

ponds to its own nature, its innate sense of harmony, to soul's or, perhaps, body's recognition of its proper habitat. In Northumberland I knew myself in my own place; and I never 'adjusted' myself to any other or forgot what I had so briefly but clearly seen and understood and experienced. I do not believe, as Wordsworth perhaps did, that the state of Paradise is childhood itself; some children have perhaps never known Paradise, or only as a longing; and some, like Blake, who claimed to be 'an inhabitant of that happy country' have found again what Wordsworth lost. Paradise is a state of being in which outer and inner reality are at one, the world in harmony with imagination. All poetry tells of that vision, all poets remember, or seek to remember and recreate what all know at heart to be not a mere fleeting illusion, but the norm we never cease to seek and to create (however often it may be destroyed) because in that state alone lies felicity. To be exiled from Eden is our greatest sorrow, and some forget, or try to forget, because to remember is too painful, to re-create too difficult. Those who choose the vision of perfection choose to experience the pain of deprivation as the lesser evil; or perhaps there is no choice. 'You are one of those who are not allowed to forget', Cecil Collins once said to me. And ultimately the many are sustained by those images of a lost perfection held before them by the rememberers. Such, as I understand it, is the whole and sole purpose of the arts and the justification of those who refuse to accept as our norm those unrealities the world calls real.

From Bavington to Ilford.

I was born at 6 Gordon Road, Ilford on the fourteenth of June, 1908; in the house where the little hand of flame danced on the gas-jet, and the world ended in a cascade of Virginia creeper beyond the hollyhocks at the bottom of our garden. On that first day—so they used to tell me—my father put into my hand a rose from my mother's Maiden's

Blush rose-bush, and my tiny fingers clasped the stem of my first flower. The poignant sweetness of the scent of that old-fashioned Alba rose has become for me the first fragrant sweetness of my mother; as a memory irrecapturable, a sweetness known before memory began.

I do not remember the house; only the garden; nor, as separate beings, my father and mother. I remember my father's bowler hat, because when at tea-time he came home from school he would give it to me, and allow me to find in the hat-band the bunch of snowdrops or violets he had hidden there; for my mother as I now suppose, but then I thought all the flowers in the world were mine.

The first event I remember is an incident which obtrudes itself, clear as a photograph, and out of context like a piece of wreckage in the clear stream of life in which my three-year-old self still floated; an event in time. I am dressed in white with a blue silk sash and hair-ribbons, carrying a little straw basket of freesias and asparagus fern. Other children, similarly attired and with little baskets of flowers, are waiting, as I am, to go onto a platform and say a poem. My mother has rehearsed me and I know my poem perfectly. She asks me to say it once more before I go on stage; and I do so. Now I must go onto the platform, and I am asked to say my poem again. This seems absurd, and I merely say 'I've said it'. There is laughter, and I am put to shame. The whole situation—the poem, the basket, the platform—is false and bewildering and I want to escape. No doubt this platform was in the hall of the Wesleyan chapel of which my father was an active member. The freesias fail to console me as I turn to their beauty as to the only beings of my own kind in this place of wooden chairs and adults.

I was three years old when we moved to West View. I remember being taken by my mother one day to look at a house. It was empty and dirty and cold and a woman care-taker showed us empty dirty rooms. Later I was told we were going to live there and dismay chilled me, as if I were going to live in an unknown house of the dead with that terrible caretaker. I remember then a day—another fragment of the ruins of time—when from the window of May's house next door I watched in woe the incessant heavy rain as strange men carried our furniture into a big removal van. Abandoned and forlorn I saw my world dismantled and gone.

Then I remember a door opening—the dining-room door of West View—and I saw my mother laughing and welcoming me. I 'saw' my mother that day for the first time, laughing and happy as she held out her arms to her little girl. The room she was in was fresh and clean, and there was a Christmas-tree, fragrant, and hung with glittering beautiful marvels, coloured glass balls and tinsel, and a soap teddy-bear and a little doll made of sugar, and twisted candles, red and blue and orange; inexhaustible, countless treasures of beauty hung on that lovely tree. Incredible transformation! The two pictures would not mix, the two houses were not the same house, but different houses; and in some inexplicable sense our new house was the same place as our old house, as if with the familiar pieces of furniture we had brought the place itself with us.

West View was still in Paradise; for with the spring the fields beyond our garden blossomed, and I, Persephone in Ida gathering flowers, astray for hours of golden eternity in the meadows and along the hawthorn hedge white with may and festooned with wild roses, first the pink, then the fragrant white Burnet rose. The various scents to my young senses were more than delight, they were indescribable harmonies of knowledge and meaning. I was, unawares, learning the scales of memory; but then memory was no longer than the length of a meadow as I ran to renew and refresh my senses with the scent of buttercups or my mother's Maiden's Blush rose, brought with her from her first garden; and there, no doubt, from Northumberland.

Memory has composed those days of my childhood into

one continuous day of late spring and early summer; in whose morning white stitchwort, white Jack-by-the-hedge with its fresh mustard scent, and white cow-parsley rose along the hedgerows, and the tight-folded small leaves of the elm trees began to open. As the sun rose higher, buttercups in their several kinds opened burnished chalices, and the sparser pale lilac cuckoo-flower. In the hawthorn hedge by the stile the first miniature green rosebuds open immaculate shell-pink petals about a golden crown, and the innumerable blossoms of the may, each petal a perfect hemisphere splashed with the coral of the young unopened anthers. Later came white marguerites—'gowans' to my mother, but not in those fields—and the ruddy sorrel changed the colour of the meadow of rising grass with its shimmering sprays, soon to fall in afternoon hay; and in the heat of the afternoon the scent of lime-blossom from the single tree that stood in the hay-meadow, where, lying in my bed in the summer evenings, I could still commune with its lovely shape. I knew where the sweet patch of summer-scented bedstraw was; and the germander speedwell, brilliant blue in the morning sun. There was no flower in these meadows whose place I did not know; from the pink bindweed on the dry gravelly hillocks of the paddock shared by a donkey and a tradesman's pony, to the single clump of king-cups in the little swampy ditch beyond the hawthorn hedge. I knew where the lark's nest was in the meadow grass, and saw in that small sanctuary first the eggs, then those naked wedge-shaped heads, all gaping beak and blind eyes. The lark that poured its song from the blue sky all those summer days was our own lark, lark of the meadow where I gathered buttercups.

My mother did not send me to school until I was six years old; and if I have been a poet I owe it to my mother's protection of my sanctuary of solitude in those years of early childhood when three small fields between the advancing fringe of London's East-End suburbs, and the wooden fence

82

of Dr. Barnardo's Homes was space enough for earthly Paradise.

I remember the day of the outbreak of war. We (for my father, my mother and I were still, when I was just six years old, 'we', an indivisible unity) were on holiday at Broadstairs. The pre-war sun shone, and there were donkey-rides on the sand. We were staying in a boarding-house; and I remember the Italian waiter, whom I loved with my whole heart, and a French family with a charming adolescent son whom I admired from the obscurity of my smallness. The sun shone on August 4th, 1914 on golden sand and the happy bathing-machine that took my mother and me out into the tepid sea water among the beautiful coral-red floating seaweed. I remember my father putting the penny into my hand to give to the paper-boy in exchange for the evening newspaper which told the news. The war had something to do with France, and the elegant French boy who would have to go back at once and who might soon have to be a soldier. I remember my mother exclaiming on 'all the men who will be killed'. To me the only sadness the war brought was parting from the Italian waiter who must have possessed the gift of so many Italians of being kind to little children.

Later, 'the war' meant tea-parties, with badminton on our garden lawn, for the 'old boys' of my father's school who came, young and gay, in khaki uniforms. It meant pretty cards from 'the trenches' embroidered with the flags of France and Belgium, and edged with French lace. It meant hanks of rough khaki knitting-wool which my mother knitted into socks and mufflers; and I too was given a pair of heavy knitting needles and set about knitting a muffler; still unfinished years after in the bottom drawer of my mother's wardrobe.

But all that was outside me; my own and only participation in 'the war' was to make little crosses by binding two sticks together with pieces of grass, and tying them to the grey feather seeds of the wild Traveller's Joy; 'for the Belgians', I said. My tribute to the dead was made without sorrow, but in a kind of ritual solemnity, impersonal as a religious rite.

On the last of childhood's timeless days I was gathering buttercups in the meadow behind the house when I heard a sound new to me, of a steady relentless humming in the air; and I looked up and saw aeroplanes approaching, with a terrible slowness; like four-winged mechanical gnats. The intensity of that sudden terror has left an imprint on my mind, like a photograph, of that moment, and the very place in the sky where I saw the enemy planes. I fled to my mother; and, as so often later, we sheltered in the cellar. I remember sometimes sleeping there, among the sacks of potatoes grown by my father on his 'allotment' just beside the house.

There were other portents in the sky in those days; I saw, from the front window of West View, the Billericay Zeppelin pass, a great pencil-like shape, and then a jet of flame, then a blaze that lit up the windows of West View. 'Are there men in it?' I asked; and when I was told 'Yes' I cried. My father told us afterwards that a dead German officer had been found by a farmer in a field, lying near his path. The man had beautiful teeth, and the farmer stamped on his face, breaking them. The Potter's Bar Zeppelin I also saw, burning in the sky, a crumpled ball of dull red fire, far away; for a long time a piece of twisted aluminium on our mantel-piece remained as a souvenir.

Which of those two Zeppelins, I now wonder, was the one Marcel saw as it passed over Paris only a few hours before I saw it burst into flames? I had been, then, only a few hours and a few miles from Marcel Proust (so I realized when long after I read his record of Paris in the war) and not only from Paris as such, but from the immortal Paris of *Le Temps Retrouvé*. Very few of the things I saw in Ilford had ever belonged, or would ever belong, to what imagination

84

retrieves from time lost; that Zeppelin was the only object besides the sun and the moon that ever crossed the horizon of West View that has its place in the annals of European literature. Yet France in those days was ever in mind; for it was to France my father's sixth-form schoolboys departed, many never to return. And the French master at the school had been a regular visitor up to that summer of 1914. I remember, not his appearance, but a quality of his presence, quick and warm and gay and intelligent, with a charming voice. He used to call me 'la petite aubépine', making me repeat the phrase until I knew my French name. Had he read those first volumes of Proust? Diffusion of culture is a strange thing; by hidden channels did my hawthorn hedge receive an added fragrance from Marcel's? My love of France, at all events, had from the beginning the scent of hawthorn.

As I think back into those years before 1914 it seems that there was something Paradisal even in Ilford itself on whose extreme outskirts we lived. In Valentine's Park, with its artificial lakes and little grotto and wishing-well, blackbirds did 'so rinse and wring the ear' in rhododendron-dells that the park seemed still the sanctuary it had once been, when its cedars were planted and its grotto by the water. In the quiet side-turnings from Cranbrook Road (called 'Redcliff Gardens' or some other 'Gardens') the only sounds were the unhurried rattle of the milkman measuring his pints, or the horse-drawn baker's van (few cars and no radio sets in those days) and the tinkling of piano-practice. To play the piano was in those days regarded as a minimal accomplishment even amongst the unmusical; but Ilford had its Metroplitan Academy of Music where the standard available to the musical children of the suburb was of the highest. The names of more than one now famous concert performer I first heard as playing in some children's concert at 'The Academy'.

West View was not in reality (as to me it seemed) a part of

85

the country beyond our garden-fence, but the advancing fringe of the tide which was already submerging the older, perhaps more cultured, certainly more leisured older strata of city merchants who built the ampler houses already, within my memory, being converted into schools and nursing homes; 'The Academy' was one such Victorian mansion in decline. There were 'educated people' just above our social horizon, some of whom my mother visited. My mother came to life, became more herself, in the company of the 'educated' (to use her own word, for in reality it was culture, not education, to which she responded) whereas my father seemed positively to seek out his social inferiors. This did not argue social ambition on her part, or humility on his: rather the reverse, for she loved to learn, he to do good to others.

There was an upright German lady who played her upright piano in a disciplined manner, whom my mother called 'the Bishopess' because she was the widow of a Moravian bishop. There was Dr. Carroll, with his immaculate white silk cravat drawn through a gold ring; there was Kendrick Pyne, a once famous cathedral organist, now retired and living with his married daughter, whose beautiful Victorian diction, whose well-turned anecdotes, had a charm of artistry peculiar to a culture now almost extinct. There were our next-door neighbours, the Websters, who had named their house (wedged between West View and number three Hamilton Gardens) 'Interim', because they were living in that small but hideous villa only between a Stock Exchange disaster and an anticipated recovery. Mr. Webster was an elegant, optimistic man, who had converted his interim garden patch into an enchanted spot with a miniature landscape of rockery and pool, gemmed with rare flowers tended with skills (some—burying, for example, a plant pot near the roots of a rare plant, to allow the water to go deeper—I remember to this day) which raised gardening to a fine art. There were besides, in that same garden, three terriers (Bobs, Jean and Lady), two cats (Satan and Tony) and a curlew with a clipped wing; which did nevertheless escape. In the front window a grey parrot in a big round cage; and a strange flask of 'bee wine' in which translucent living globules rose and sank in a truly marvellous manner. There were several handsome grown-up sons and daughters, and Gwen, a few years older than I, with whom I played. Mrs. Webster had white frizzed hair fitting her head like a cap, or the powdered hair of the eighteenth century; she wore an enamelled gold watch pinned to the fastidiously clean elaborate lace-trimmed corsage of her blouse. I could not have said wherein it was that the Webster's way of life was not as ours; I only knew that life 'next door' was as rich and full of marvels as the Arabian Nights. It was 'fun'; quite useless things were done for their own sake. That pre-war sense of play never visited my parents' house; no conversational grey parrot delighted us by occasionally laying a round white useless egg; none of the gay bursts of song and litter of bric-à-brac of the money-spinning Websters. My parents took money very seriously and literally (my father from the working-class, my mother from parsimonious Scotland) and there was an intangible atmosphere of moral disapproval of those gay Websters who did not take money seriously. Unfortunately for the moral my father might have liked to draw, that happy circus did in due course return to the world from which it had so cheerfully descended. Interim was occupied by an elementary schoolmaster with false teeth and a small boy with a squint and spectacles. Respectability's heavy shadow fell as frivolity departed.

Even my infants' school was Paradisal. 'Miss Hutchinson's school' in The Drive was just a large house with a garden at the back where we used to feed the tortoise with leaves from the Lombardy poplar; from which it delighted us by taking clear-cut wedge-shaped bites. We made delightful little boxes out of coloured paper, embroidering them in patterns laid out for us in dots whose traces we had but to follow to create things of beauty such as we could never have imagined ourselves capable of. I could of course read before I went to school; and the weekly award of 'the button' went either to me or to a boy called Alan Prior whose handsome person I much admired. There were two beautiful ash-fair boys, twins—a magical relationship—called Brian and Willow Mackay. For some forgotten reason—perhaps because he was not good at his lessons, being delicate, or with the amoral cruelty of the healthy for the ailing—we teased poor Willow; and when, after a period of absence from school we were told that Willow was dead, there was already guilt mingled with my evanescent childish sorrow.

My second school—the Highlands Elementary School—was not in Paradise; a red-brick prison in an asphalt play-ground, where in encaustic-tiled classrooms sixty little girls sat at desks before a blackboard. What we learned from the blackboard I do not remember; but I do remember an episode—another piece of human wreckage polluting the stream of life—which shook me deeply. A pretty, precocious dark girl (she afterwards became a professional dance hostess) had been naughty in some way of which I have no memory. Much tried as she must have been in her daily struggle to control a class of sixty, our Miss Smith's usually mild temper broke, and she called dark Gwenyth to stand out in front of the class and hold out her hands for the cane. Caning was rare, at least among seven-year-olds; and the sentence struck at my life in an indescribable way. I shook and trembled uncontrollably as I sat with lowered eyes so as not to see the awful punishment carried out. Gwenyth had spirit and showed less dread than I. When the class was dismissed Miss Smith kept me back; she spoke to me as an equal, asking me if I thought she had done wrong. That a grown-up ever could do wrong had not occurred to me; and so I said, 'Oh no'; but that it had seemed such a very terrible thing to happen. My reaction was not moral, had

88

nothing to do with justice or injustice; it was the sense of the deep dreadfulness of punishment, as if the person punished could never be the same again, would bear the scar for ever. I do not any longer know just what it was I did feel then; for nearly sixty years in this world have dulled my realization, which was then so absolute, that some violations are irreparable. Perhaps all punishment, then, had for me the awfulness of the divine punishment for sin, eternal condemnation, a judgement passed on the soul of the sinner against which there is no appeal. For I did not for a moment doubt that Gwenyth had done something very wrong, or that her punishment was just. I do not remember a time when I did not know that we must walk a knife-edge between right and wrong, and that one sin was enough to blemish the original perfection, the sinlessness of childhood. For such was the Puritan morality which hoped for each child a sinless life; seeing sin not as the human condition into which all are born, all alike sinners who need forgiveness continually; but as a series of specific acts which we must on no account commit. Girls with illegitimate babies, drunkards and the like, were as a matter of course thrown out of non-conformist chapels (and according to Thomas Hardy also from the Church of England) in those days, and morality was a continual effort to preserve virtue and to avoid, not so much sin, as 'sins'. As a child I was resolved never to sin. The contempt of these moral athletes for Catholics who would 'confess to a priest' and then light-heartedly sin the very next day was boundless; but, however sincere, the effort not to 'sin' concealed a blindness to the human situation and the real nature of good and evil. I did make friends—fascinated and venturing out of my depth—with Gwenyth after that episode; but always with the fearful knowledge that my friend was not one of the good, but one of the bad; like Hans Andersen's robber-girl.

I remember yet another, more poignant occasion; a very abject, probably poor and rather dirty unattractive little girl sobbing and tear-stained, with no handkerchief to wipe away the repulsive grime melted in tears and making her face ugly, sobbing out 'It's my *birthday*'. I felt this to the heart; for a birthday was a day inviolable, a day which belonged to each child as their very identity. If even an ugly dirty little girl could be caned on her birthday, where was justice, where was sanctuary? Some sanctities go deeper than questions of right and wrong; and there was not a seven-year-old among us who did not feel, as I did, that a great wrong had been done against childhood's birthright.

From Bavington I have few memories of books or fantasies, for I had no need of these where the world was itself the region of imagination in which I moved. But in Ilford the two worlds must early have diverged; for whereas all I remember from Northumberland is of the sensible world, nearly all from Ilford which I have not either forgotten or rejected is of dreams and fantasies, and of certain stories which had over me the magical power of dreams.

A fantasy which companioned me for a long time must come from before the years when I lived with Aunty Peggy Black at the manse. Going to bed by day, in summer, I passed the hours before sleep in the other world. Not in dream but in waking fantasy I would take off, from the bed where I lay, to the summits of some beautiful heavy elms I could see from my window which grew a field away, by a little stream, or ditch rather, which gathered in a pool where by day I watched sticklebacks, water-boatmen, water-snails, planaria, and occasionally beautiful newts, and all manner of strange lives. From the pool the water flowed away under a brick culvert into darkness and mystery; and down into that mystery, each evening, I passed, travelling with the speed of thought to 'the bottom of the sea'.

There my companion awaited me: an octopus. How came I by that fantasy? I know only that it was so, and that among the mysteries under the sea we travelled together in perfect identity of thought. I did not need Plato to tell me

90

that the 'real' world is a pale reflection of the divine originals stored in those inaccessible treasuries.

A lifetime later I read in Jung's *Aion* of the era of the Fish, and of a round fish, known to the alchemists, dwelling at the bottom of the sea, whose powers are marvellous and whose strength can stop ships in their course. The round magic-working fish seemed to me as I read a symbol so uncouth and improbable that I was about to dismiss the account as having, for me, no imaginable meaning, when there came flooding back (as if I had eaten a crumb of magic *madeleine* dipped in lime-flower tisane) the memory of my long-forgotten octopus; a world. What the octopus meant, or was, or the round fish of the Alchemists, I do not know; but clearly others who have been where I was, have there found the same mental beings.

That night I dreamed of the octopus; no longer as a living *alter ego*, but as a lifeless diagram, a mathematical demonstration; but one last communication of wisdom my octopus gave me before vanishing for ever. The eight arms formed themselves, as I looked, with a kaleidoscopic shift, into the shape of a Maltese cross. What did the octopus mean by that shape-shifting, that transmutation of the wild hidden life of the abyss into the world-ruling emblem which so ambiguously combines the peace of Christ with the sign of the Enemy warrior, the Iron Cross of the First World War which was the background of my childhood? So astonished was I that I sent an account of my dream and the earlier fantasy to a Jungian psychiatrist whom I had lately met, saying that this confirmation of his symbol might please Dr. Jung; who himself wrote in reply that my fantasy was a sign of 'the chosen one'—such was his phrase. He spoke of 'a pair of friends like Mithras and Helios or Kastor and Pollux or Chadir and Elijah etc.' and 'the hero who recognizes the Dragon to be himself'. Those born, as I am, under the sign of Gemini, have often, I believe, a very strong sense of their other self, the immortal daimon who accompanies every mortal. It is said of the Dioscuri that one is mortal, the other immortal; and in that sign the poet and his guide walk hand in hand, we here, they there, in un-interrupted communion. Dante was of that sign, and Yeats (my birthday is between theirs, on June 14th). My sense of an accompanying daimon (though not in octopus-form) has been with me all the years of my poetry; but who in so strange a shape would have recognized a companion akin to Dante's Virgil or Yeats's Instructors?

As a child I had known that I was a 'chosen one'; I never doubted it. Perhaps all souls are chosen-ones, though not all awakened to self-knowledge. Certainly there was nothing competitive in my sense of vocation; for vocation differs from ambition in that it concerns no one but ourselves; it is secret; its obligations, being self-imposed, are inescap-able. I had no wish to excel, or to surpass or to be admired; my task concerned no one but myself; the children with whom I played knew nothing of my inner life, in which they played no part. I felt neither superior, inferior, nor anything at all in relation to them; children do not make comparisons, things are as they are.

My land-under-wave is confused in my memory with the story of *The Little Mermaid*; perhaps my fantasy took its form from that story; or it may have been the other way, and my deep sense of identity with Hans Andersen's mermaid may have come from the archetypal character of that land-under-wave,

> The Mind, that Ocean where each kind
> Does straight its own resemblance find;
> Yet it creates, transcending these,
> Far other Worlds and other Seas.

But I would have no marble statue of a prince in my garden of coral and sea-flowers! No, indeed—for who would exchange the ecstasy of freedom, of plunging beneath the waves, of drifting on the surface of beautiful seas, a world of life inexhaustible, for so finite a passion as love? Not I! With troubled sorrow I read of her visit to the witch-woman, who demanded the tongue with which she sang so sweetly as the price of the mixed potion which should change her fish's tail into a pair of feet to walk the earth, every step a pain as if she walked on knives; of the dumbness of the soul that cannot speak its knowledge to earthly ears; and the ending I then thought sad beyond endurance. For the Mermaid, who failed to win the love of her prince, must be transmuted yet again, this time into a spirit of the air, with a far hope of winning immortality. As a child I could scarcely bear to read that ending; but now, near the end of the unfolding pattern, I am grateful for the story, which tells, in symbols so charming, the deep truth of the soul's pilgrimage. Perhaps we each instinctively recognize, among the countless possibilities of fancy, the pattern of our own life.

Another story of land-under-wave that then enthralled me was Kingsley's *Water-Babies*; and above all the journey to the North, under the wall of ice, to that pool where in a great calm the creatures are created, gull and tern and gannet and fulmar and shearwater, for ever and ever uprising on wings of immortal life in its myriad forms. Yet another was La Motte Fouqué's *Undine*, whose lover came to her as the rain beat and the torrent cut off the fisherman's cottage from the world with streaming sounding cataracts. That story too had an ending too dreadful to be borne; even on the great navigable river of her descent from Paradise the fairy bride could still dip her arm into the water and bring up pearls and jewels for her knight; but in the world of men and women to which at last they came, he forgot her; no longer 'saw' her; no longer remembered; until, led away unwillingly by her own people, back into the world of spirits, bitterly weeping, she was compelled to leave her knight, married, like the Mermaid's sleeping prince, to a mortal wife; and he sealed his fountain with a stone, lest through it she might rise again. But at the end the fountain, as it must be, was unsealed; and from it the Undine rose, weeping; slowly, reluctantly, she went to Hildebrand, he too weeping now with the clouded joy of love remembered too late. Folding him in her cold reluctant arms, she was the unwilling messenger of death. But why, I felt then, did he forget her, his true love, how could he turn from the greater love to the less, from the supernatural to the natural bride? And how could the Mermaid's prince be so blind as not to understand that it was she, not the commonplace earth-born princess, who had carried him in her arms to the shores of his kingdom? Why? And to this day I have not understood why the mortal sleep must fall upon us, when once we have glimpsed immortal beauty.

West View was the last—or first—of a row of three brick houses in the style of 1908. There were two patterns in Ilford, double-fronted and single-fronted; our house was double-fronted, the dining-room window on one side of the front door, the drawing-room on the other. Over each of these rooms was a bedroom, and over each bedroom a 'Tudor' gable. Long ago these houses were swallowed up in the no-man's land which advanced into Essex, between the two wars, to meet the needs of a population multiplying with a like rapidity. But as I first remember it our house stood at the very extreme boundary, and I, a country child, could still find in the buttercup meadows and the pasture field beyond our wooden creosoted garden fence the world I recognized, nature immaculate. The house really, then, had a West View; from the front windows we could watch the sun slowly setting over misty fields bordered with pollarded elms; 'Essex Maidens' they were called, for their slender beauty, crowned with a delicate chevelure of leaves. Our own elms, one standing in our garden, and its companions across the country road (the end of an avenue which continued towards the village of Barkingside) were not pollarded, but such hedgerow elms as Milton might have loved. Only on summer Saturdays were we reminded of the nearness of London, but in a manner that would have delighted Blake himself. In the morning, the heavy clatter of horses' hooves would approach, and the sound of brisk singing; charabancs higher than any farm-cart but in the same idiom as Constable's drays and hay-wains, full of children and their elders from the East End, were on their way to some Sunday School treat in Epping forest. There were, as a rule, several of these top-heavy joyous waggons. One would approach with its happy clatter and jingle and singing, and before its crescendo had died away into a diminuendo, the next would come, pass, and go; and the next; four or five charabancs. In the evening they would return, at a slower pace, all hung with green bracken, branches of forest trees, and big bunches of flowers from Essex cottage gardens; cabbage roses and madonna lilies and pinks hanging like votive garlands all round the sides. The singing now was sleepy, sentimental and harmonious; the major key of morning hope modified into an evening *raga* as the children and their elders, drowsy with sunshine, fulfilment and the long drive home, returned, sated with country pleasures. But after the war the great 'development' of Essex began. Our country road was tarred now, and the charabancs disappeared along with the high farm-carts with their woodwork painted in red and blue and yellow visible under the mud of turnips and potatoes, the milk-cart and the baker's cart with their little ponies. There began to be cars, though at first not many.

Then a 'bus service was opened. An open-topped omnibus (so it was still called) turned round under the last elm of the avenue, a few yards from our door. The top seats were often wet and you pulled a canvas cover over your knees to keep the rain off. The branches swished over you as the 'bus made its way townwards; some of the overhanging boughs of the trees along the route were lopped off on this account. I remember the mutiliated tree at the 'bus-stop, with its great scar where the branch had been sawn away, and my father's explanation, in terms of safety and utility, of the mutilation of the tree's life and beauty. My father's answers never quite fitted my questions; the good was, for us, situated differently, his in social improvement, mine in the beautiful and the integrity of nature. Elms, so he told me, are 'dangerous'; sometimes their branches fall; what if this were to happen when someone was standing underneath? I did not put into words my real thought on the matter; but not only did this seem to me extremely improbable, but by far the lesser evil, man being more common and less noble than great elms. I knew such thoughts to be, by Christian standards, wicked, but remained rebellious; for there was the scar: the tree it was that died.

But our own lovely elm was safe meanwhile, and those opposite, their lace-like dusky leaves heaped in cumulus-forms. At their foot the hedgerow plants flourished, white stitch-wort, white Jack-by-the-hedge, white foam of cow-parsley. Even so near London people still walked along country roads enjoying green hedges and birds and flowers. We are only within the world of nature (created with and for man, whether by miracle or by natural adaptation) when we are on foot; cars do not take us 'into' the country but out of it; out of nature altogether, for to see flying fields and hedges is not to be in them. My own lifetime has seen the destruction of a companionship of ages.

Higher up the road, towards the village, a manor-house stood in its deserted garden; of the period of Queen Anne, as it now seems to me. I remember thinking the mellow brick house with its broad windows very beautiful, standing in its pleasant grounds where cedars of Lebanon laid their flat branches low over the sweep of the lawn. Into that magic ground, that forsaken garden, I, with other children, timidly trespassed; climbed on those low branches and marvelled at the great cedar-cones. I sensed a *genius loci* strange indeed to me, the *genius* of the gentry; of the eighteenth century behind the nineteenth, like a vista. Nature here was refined, enhanced; here bluebells grew larger and finer than those in the woods; flowering shrubs whose names I did not know; a great hedge of sweet-briar. I had never before seen a place made beautiful by man, whom I knew better as a destroyer of beauty. The barriers between social classes were then indeed *barricades mysterieuses*; I knew that I had trespassed, had crossed an invisible barrier when I breathed the scent of cedar on that deserted lawn. I did not know it as a barrier of class or caste, but I sensed a richer and more beautiful, a less abject world, and felt drawn towards it by a kind of nostalgia for something that ought to be. I was not the only trespasser, but only a drop in a rising tide; for the deserted manor was to be pulled down; a building estate was to take its place; development, it was called: an experience, at all events, to be undergone, though a moment only in the endless metamorphosis of the world.

Our elms, too, were to go; the road had already been widened and their roots undermined. But before the fellers began their work there came a storm in the night with wind, rain, thunder, and lightning. In the morning four elms had fallen, their roots standing up in the air, their delicate leafy heads laid low. I remember how empty that piece of sky looked, a blank light that hurt the eyes. Where something had been there was a nothing haunted by their absence.

At first I half hoped that if I went to sleep and woke again, the trees would be back in their accustomed places. Spring, besides, set about its gentle task of healing the earth's wounds. The cleavers and Jack-by-the-hedge formed themselves to the new pattern, growing lush and tall by the fallen trunks. But then came men with saws and lopped off the great branches until only the trunks remained; then these, too, were gone, and the remaining elms (their torn shapes never mended to their broken sky) put, as it were, out of their misery and felled too. Then there was a time of bricks and gravel, hammering and scraping, until a row of mean shops stood in the way of our West View. At the corner, where the brick wall of the old manor demesne still hid its doomed garden, stood a sweetshop-tobacconist; then a United Dairy, kept by a greasy pig-like woman in a dirty uniform; then an ironmonger's and domestic stores kept by a strangely repulsive man, with a silent wife who sometimes hovered behind the dark counter. Her profile was fine and delicate and her abundant coils of pre-Raphaelite auburn hair gave her the dignity of beauty. She committed suicide within a year or two. To me her choice of death seemed wise and noble; to live in a mean flat above that shop with its smell of chemical products tied to so vile a man, was reason enough to drive her to the one way of escape open to such prisoners. Next, I think, came a grocer's, then a wool and needlework shop that sold odds and ends of baby clothes, stockings and the like. The unreal and the mean had moved like a nightmare into a place that had seemed as enduring as seed time and harvest, summer and winter, day and night.

To say I grieved is needless; but besides grief there had already begun to grow in me indignation and disgust and outrage and misanthropy; bitterly, but not with childhood's innocent grief, I lamented the usurpation of the beautiful world by the mean, the meaningless and the vulgar. The mean, meaningless and vulgar being was man. That transformation which I was to watch, day by day, week by week, month by month in that doomed Essex countryside has left its desolation upon me. Never have I become reconciled; the nameless nomads who swarmed into the new building estates which seemed to have arisen overnight, and as if in a nightmare, seemed to me then—and to this day it requires an effort of will to rectify the judgement—something quite other than the humanity of which I read in those books which (so the end-pages of a famous edition constantly reminded readers of my generation) are 'the life-blood of a master spirit'. Where did they come from? Who were they?

Their speech was scarcely articulate, like the voices of the ghosts in Hades; they were too frightened, those timid swarms, to raise their voices. Their only refinement was a paralysis of fear; their lives were apologetic, as though they themselves doubted their right to exist. They seemed to have come from nowhere; not from any place that could be called a place; not from the Essex villages, where pinks and cabbages grew in untidy fertility. Having no past they seemed to have, even for themselves, no identity, nor could they impart any reality to the new dream into which the wind of time had blown them.

Not real people at all, I felt; not like Grannie Carr, who in her dark stone cottage set her good loaves to rise on the polished steel kitchen fender; and who in the corner cupboard kept her Wedgwood dishes, an heirloom like the d'Urberville's worn silver spoon, a link with the ways of life and values of an eighteenth-century English civilization not yet extinct in her cottage. Not like the farmers' daughters, who were my merry play-fellows, climbing among the hay in the barn to see the swallows' nests; not even like the village outcast, Bella, at The Mires cottage, with her fatherless children; who at times would repent and come to church, and sit behind those sweet, narrow Presbyterian farmers' wives with their tall Northumbrian figures upright in the varnished pews. They were not real like my father's poorer people; Aunt Marie and Aunt Sally with their village post office and the little dark shop smelling of yeast where the miners' wives and dirty children came, often without money to pay; and for the love of God Aunt Marie would often give them what they could not buy. Yet even those people had an identity, a past, a place however humble. My father's father, whose life was the religion taught to his grandfather by John Wesley, was proud of his tradition; proud of Durham cathedral, the cathedral of those earlier Raines who had been country people living in Teesdale.

Did those people only seem thus unreal because they had

moved into a place which had no roots in the past, no function in relation to the earth upon which it had risen? Or was that formless proliferation of low-class suburbia perhaps the expression rather than the cause of that loss of identity, of orientation either social or spiritual? The Essex Maidens, the white foam of cow-parsley, the muddy lanes bordering misty ploughed fields, farms with walnut trees, chestnut avenues, all that old slowly traced, slowly matured human pattern of life lived from generation to generation was gone in less time than the sowing, reaping and harvesting of a field of corn. The new pattern no longer bore any relationship to shelter of hill or fall of stream; fertile and barren were alike to speculative builders. Then an arterial road advanced from London, severing like a cut artery the beginning of a lane, bordered with bramble and hawthorn, bleeding away now into the cement and gravel of the ribbon-building which sprawled endlessly in roads leading nowhere. As cancer cells proliferate without the informing pattern of the life of a human body, so this new way of life proliferated, cell by cell, rapidly killing the life of villages and old farms and parishes and manor houses. I knew that something was taking place all round me which I wanted to stop, for all seemed wrong about it, as if it were some vast mistake, beyond control. Who was making this mistake I did not know; but reading its lineaments I knew its meaning. What it told in its form, or lack of form, was something immeasurably evil, if evil be not too grandiose a word for the apathetic negation of the past of the earth and all the memories of man. It was as if the earth were being killed; and humanity becoming something quite other than that for which man was created, upon that earth now stricken. Or rather, not becoming anything, only unbecoming, ceasing to be something and becoming an unreality so immense that my young soul's 'No, No' was as powerless against it as the lark's song or the petals of a wild rose opening in a doomed hedgerow. My father saw in it human progress; in the L.C.C. houses, housing for 'the people'; easy for the theorizers to dismiss the here and now, but those who prove life on their pulses are usually less fortunate. I saw with incredulous sorrow a desolation deliberately created. My mother refused to see it at all; that was how the poet in her kept faith with what should have been.

That I belonged to the same species as those who came to live in the little mean houses and shops springing up all round us, I no more realized than Mowgli in his jungle knew himself to be a man. I realize now how little I knew of the lives of these suburb-dwellers, with whom we never mixed. Behind their garden fences and little front gates which bore each its declaration of the privacy of what lay beyond on a little enamel plate with the words 'No hawkers, no circulars', the women hovered, keeping their lives hidden. The men, dressed in dark suits and bowler hats, left each morning for their mysterious 'offices' in 'the City' (reached in the packed coaches of steam trains to Liverpool Street) and returned each evening to enter their small foothold of safety, or whatever else was theirs behind the ring-pass-not of those garden fences protected by their enamel talismans, 'No hawkers, no circulars'. These indeed bore the only clue to their desires: to find sanctuary, somewhere, from the pursuit of a bewildering impersonal and hostile world. Behind their privet hedges they tended their little bright-green lawns, carefully uprooting dandelion or daisy; no weed grew among the straight rows of bright-coloured flowers, lobelia and geraniums and marguerites and, in the midst of the garden, a 'standard' bush of the Daily Mail or some other rose of the same vivid leathery kind. That was before their dreams, growing less timid, relaxed into crazy-paving, aubretia and Darwin tulips. Those stiff little plots seem, in retrospect, idyllic in comparison with the machines which have drawn them away from even that diminished Eden. The car, symbol of total displacement, and the television set, symbol of the universal invasion of the sanctuary, have banished the Daily Mail rose, the suburban Tree of Life.

Perhaps in my sense of exile, of belonging elsewhere—of belonging, above all, not *there*—I was after all not so much exceptional as typical of that place. Those tenuous and inarticulate lives must have come from somewhere, must have brought some sense of memory of an identity and a past.

In that world dreams unattainable were nourished upon the easily attainable; the powders and creams that will make the woman beautiful; the insurance policy which will give the wage-slave, in his old age (but they do not say old age; they say, 'retirement') the freedom denied him by the very nature of his life. They hoped, yet did not hope, expected, but did not expect, the realization of dreams. What they would never relinquish was the dream itself; without those dreams they would indeed be lost.

Here was neither the realism nor the poetry of the feudal world; for these dispossessed people had no conception of the ways of life of other sections of society. They did not indeed belong to an integrated society at all which could be said to have other sections. There was no flow either out of, nor into, their lives, of anything greater, or other, than themselves; only the mirage of affluence created for them by the popular press and those advertisements which for them took on the dimensions and even the function of a mythology. People of higher classes they envisaged not in terms of what these thought, or did, or were, for of those realities they knew nothing, but solely in terms of what they owned; owned in terms readily translated into currency.

Different indeed from the people I had known, who participated in the whole hierarchy of which they formed a part. This is perhaps the worst deprivation of the society called 'classless'; all is alike and all is lowered to the level of the masses who comprise it. Rich and poor, great and small no longer know one another, no longer enrich one another's lives.

But Ilford harboured more passionate dreams; there was Mrs. Thompson and her adolescent sailor lover, both hanged for his stabbing of her husband within yards of his own privet hedge; so ended a love far beyond their means, beyond the narrow scope and meagre possibility of lower middle-class suburban life; a love, one might say, above their station; for in these two the flame of life burned too brightly for Ilford, whose apathetic and timid average created a context in which their tragedy became all too explicable. Many must have dreamed what they enacted. Murder was a crime altogether apart, unimaginable; murderers were no longer like other human beings, but quite cast out and cast away. But no one seemed to understand what I remember chiefly feeling at the time of the Ilford murder, how appalling a thing it is for a man to have rights of possession over the body of a woman, young, in love; the anguish of that desecration I felt (as once the death of a farm beast) in every fibre of my own young body; I too might (so I then thought) have been driven to murder to rid myself of a possession so outrageous, against nature. Even now I find it difficult to imagine or believe that there may be women who do not mind so very much being bound in a loveless marriage; a majority, perhaps, who would find the violence of my own (and Edith Thompson's) revulsion equally inconceivable; that anyone could care so much. Blake (but I did not know about Blake in those days) would have understood how, for such enslaved Daughters of Albion, an intolerable marriage becomes a prison from which the only release is some passionate dream or fantasy, whose enactment—for such fantasies are never meant to be enacted—brings tragedy; suicide, murder, hanging. Had I not been a poet, one of these might have been my fate also; the wife of the iron-monger found with her beautiful head of pre-Raphaelite hair in a cheap gas-stove, *c'est moi*; Edith Thompson, *c'est moi*: that privet hedge in Kensington Gardens grew within a stone's throw of the Cranbrook Park Wesleyan Methodist

103

Church, and the Highlands Elementary School playground, shades of my own prison house.

My father looked for no earthly happiness; he, and his father, and his father's father, had known that man in this world is 'a stranger and a sojourner'; all he asked was to perform the task of his life—and for him life was precisely that, a task to be performed—sure of the reward of the faithful servant in another world. 'Well done, thou good and faithful servant!'; these were the words he most wished to hear. Of his safe homecoming to Heaven he had no doubt; he lived at peace with God. Therefore, for the brief time to be spent in this world, Ilford was as good a place as another to serve his Master in. 'Whatsoever thy hand findeth to do, do it with all thy might' was a text he loved to repeat. Ambition had no place in his life; was, indeed, unimaginable to him, for he did not regard his life as his own; only as his Master's. He could never, I think, envisage any other way of conceiving a life given by God. If he had a fault it was in a sort of stubborn pride he took in his refusal to be ambitious, in his too resolute adherence to the humblest tasks. Humility can be a form of evasion; and perhaps an excessive respect for humility made him unaware of other virtues. He was proud to tell how his father had always refused promotion, though a poor miner, even to the rank of foreman; for as a Christian he had felt it wrong to hold office over his fellows. These virtues suited not only my father's religion, but also his temperament, for he was not, like my mother, or like me, driven by a desire for perfection, for the beautiful, for boundless joy and wild freedom. He liked to recount the triumphs as a student, when he came first in every examination he ever took, from the time he was a pupil-teacher in his village school, to his degrees at Durham University; but at that time coming first in examinations was a task assigned, and therefore and only therefore to be done with all his might. I could never please him; for if I ever came top in examinations (I seldom did, but I tried) it was not as a duty to be performed but because I was carried away by the beauty of geometry, poetry, or plant-forms. Whatever I have achieved—little enough—only, I think, made my father ashamed of me; for earthly glory, even the smallest trace of it, is a departure from the egalitarianism of 'primitive Christianity' as he conceived it. To him the paradox never presented itself by which, in the very act of embodying some vision of the beautiful, glory and earthly splendour are inevitably created. Yet he loved cathedrals and above all Durham Cathedral: his own. Perhaps he was not wrong in caring only for such art as expressed a vision beyond all human greatness, an art expressing the glory not of man but of his maker; Plato, after all held much the same view of art. Where he was perhaps wrong was in supposing 'the good', in a moral sense, to be possible in the absence of such expressions, which are the flowering of its own vitality, and the language in which alone immaterial values are communicable.

My mother never cared for what she called 'the daily round, the common task'; that was her way of putting 'Whatsoever thy hand findeth to do . . .'. As a little girl on the moors her favourite books had been the *Scottish Chiefs* and *The Arabian Nights Entertainments*; a child's version, no doubt, but nothing can expurgate from those stories the thirst for luxury and the beauties and marvels of the world. Perhaps in Milton too she responded to the nostalgia for the earthly paradise Comus offered and Eve lost. But when I knew her, her unsatisfied longing for life's joys and marvels had retreated into the vivid dreams in which she lived night after night; dreams and her flower-garden. She loved poetry because it alone answered to her insatiable longing for beauty and wonder. My father, on the contrary, loved poetry chiefly for its 'message' (for him its 'message' was not its beauty) and, as he often assured my mother, with perhaps a shade too much complacency, he 'never dreamed'.

Of Shelley's adolescent and vague political idealism my father approved, and on that account forgave him his entranced lovers sailing in their magic boats. But he loved also the *Ode to the West Wind*, whose 'message' for him, was the harnessing of that 'impetuous one' in the cause of 'the people'; for him the new birth to be quickened was socialism; Christianity in practice, as he saw it.

My father despised Ilford's lowest of the lower middle-class suburb-dwellers precisely because these were not, in his sense, 'the people'. They were not low enough; they were, in his eyes, little better than those abstractions 'the capitalists' for they too worked in order to 'make money', and to buy all manner of 'things' ('things are in the saddle, and ride the world' was another favourite quotation). He truly believed that if 'the people' ruled, universal brotherhood would prevail; he thought 'the people' free from all those vices they had lacked the means to satisfy; mistaking the enforced poverty of the lowest social class for the freely chosen 'holy poverty' of the saints. So he taught English literature and Latin to the sons of Ilford city clerks and commercial travellers, using both as vehicles for his 'message' in the spirit of a missionary among the heathen. He despised these suburban-dwellers because they did not live by any values above those of self-interest; and he missed, in that unoriented world, a certain reality which he had known among his own people; a truth of feeling and a fervour of religion found only, perhaps, where sudden death is, as in the coal-mines, a daily possibility. It is one of the paradoxes no social reformer has resolved, that to make living conditions materially easier does not improve the quality of the people themselves; in some respects the opposite. So my father refused tenaciously—perhaps too tenaciously—to 'rise' in society, or, rather, to admit that he had done so. What he refused to see was that when, in his new M.Litt. gown and furred hood, he had walked across the close of Durham University, he had already left that world; a process which, once begun, cannot be reversed, or arrested, perhaps, for many generations; until the new growth has reached its term. I must have been three years old when I saw my father, looking, as I now realize, both young and happy in his academic dress, crossing that ancient close. Durham with its cathedral and its university was not yet, in those days, 'red brick', but the city of the old Bishops Palatine, the city of the sons of County Durham, even the poorest of them, the miners. My grandfather was there; the city of Bede and Cuthbert was his city and the city of his forefathers. Even miners, then, remembered the valleys whence their fathers had come. It was my grandfather (and who had a better right than he?) who held me up in his arms to touch the sanctuary knocker with its lion's head, with the strange hollow eye-sockets and solar mane; he it was who told me, then or later, that anyone, no matter what crime he had committed, had but to reach that door and lay his hand upon that knocker; to be safe from the pursuit of his enemies; for the Cathedral was a sanctuary; in it all could find refuge. To the door of Christian refuge my grandfather's arms lifted me.

My mother, I think, felt herself to be living in that make-shift suburb only provisionally—only 'for now'. Even in Northumberland she had lived, a race-proud Scot, as a stranger, refusing to identify herself in any way with the English; and as the daughter of a Scotch mother I too refused to be 'English'. On my mother, besides, words acted like a spell of enchantment, and the name 'West View' made her continue to believe even when the United Dairy and the domestic stores closed our earthly view, that our mis-shapen windows looked out towards the sunset and the golden country beyond the sunset. She retreated into her dreams and into her flowers. There was a China rose that covered the back of the house (of yellow brick and of a not displeasing simplicity) with its long, strong-thorned branches and clusters of exquisite shell-petalled double roses.

I have never seen its kind anywhere since, and think of it as perhaps grown from a cutting taken in some garden before suburbia usurped the land; perhaps from the deserted manor-house of Gearies. Nothing of the new desolation which had usurped the view and the fields to which she had first come to live was, for my mother, ever really there. Those mean new houses spreading over mile after mile of earth laid waste had indeed an air of the impermanent, the provisional, the make-shift; or of that kind of unreality we meet in dreams, in which a place we know is unlike itself. From dreams we wake and the illusion passes; but as day succeeded day this outrage of an earlier memory, a former aspect of things, this defacement did not fade. So, imperceptibly, my mother's life itself diverged from reality; like a road that forks, at first, only a little, but at last leads us far out of our way.

Since my mother did not, ever, really live in that place, or in those days which succeeded one another without awakening to remove the desolation from before her eyes, she began to neglect her appearance. At eighteen—I have a photograph taken of her then—she was poignantly beautiful, tall, with the proud sweet charm of her race. At twenty-eight she was still so; but tamed. Little by little she ceased to care; her dresses—it was a long time before she stopped dressing as if for her native moors—would 'do for now'; and so with her cups and dishes and her furniture. Even the meals she set before us were provisional; they too, were good enough for the time being; but the loaf on the table at Bavington and the eggs, and the milk new from the cow had been the thing itself, in a here and now which never or seldom, any more, seemed to reach us in that non-time and non-place. For what now, and here, my mother was waiting she could not have said; indeed she may not have known that she was waiting, only that these days were to be lived through; not lived in. Gradually she lost some of the freshness of her Scottish speech, for lack of those with

108

whom to speak her own language. Yet I believe her lost paradise was an earthly one; she was never content to be, like my father, 'a stranger and a sojourner' in this world. She had, as I had (and I owed mine to her, to my being her child) known the wild joy of freedom. She subscribed, of course, to my father's religious principles; and yet to her life they never seemed appropriate, as they were to his. Eve among the thorns and thistles remembered the past; Adam looked towards the future: but I too was a daughter of Eve.

Every morning, after breakfast—and in recent years I have found myself falling into the same habit—my mother would walk round her garden, teapot in hand, from flower to flower, seeing what buds had opened each day, or bulbs appeared above the soil. The tea-leaves would be given to a fern before she returned to her household tasks, which she disliked; she never ceased to protest against the necessity of having to do them; she developed a resentful perfectionism, but without ever, in a long lifetime, becoming tamed to a way of life from which she never thought of attempting to escape, because no other came within her range of possibility. That round of her garden was a brief return to Paradise; she had come to terms with exile in her own way, refusing to see what lay beyond her flowers. My ever-living protest continually broke across her own way of being reconciled to her life. Refusing to see what her West View had become, she could not bear me to remind her of the surrounding desolation; she must build her refuge or have none; but I, being young, meant to escape. I knew that I was not where I belonged or with my own people; and each day I refused the proffered pomegranate. I had not needed to realize that what I felt still to be my place was no longer mine; for Bavington was still there, my Aunty Peggy lived on at the manse. But in the years that followed in the struggle to keep faith with my earliest vision of the beauty and the truth of nature, I became involved in a cruel and continuous battle against my new environment and, finally, with my parents, who attempted to hold me to the world which they had made theirs, or which had, in the end, made them captive.

My father used with me only one argument of persuasion to accept Ilford: religion. Christian charity demands that we love our neighbours (neighbours! my heart said, these are not *my* neighbours). Yet his own love for mankind was remote and idealistic; he attempted to educate the sons of those suburb-dwellers in the spirit of a missionary; to have liked them as they were would have seemed to him a betrayal of his ideal of 'humanity' as it should be; a perfection as remote and vague as the choruses of *Prometheus Unbound*. When he found that I shared his contempt for the actual, while refusing to dedicate myself to the service of the ideal humanity, he was displeased and troubled. Poetry, too, which he himself had encouraged me to read, was a cause of division; for him a means to an end (the betterment of mankind) for me poetry seemed rather one of the ends to which humanity was perhaps only the means.

In loyalty to his father and his father's father he had remained a Methodist; and now, instead of the sweet staid sabbaths of Bavington my mother and I were led, she unwillingly but dutiful, I unwillingly and protesting, to the Cranbrook Park Wesleyan Methodist Church (it was not called a chapel, for the Cranbrook Park congregation had aspirations) every Sunday morning and evening. My father never doubted but that in time he would by patience and his own unswerving conviction of what was right, bring my mother to share his dearest beliefs; that I would do so he took for granted. That my mother remained uninterested troubled and puzzled him, but he never for a moment asked himself why this might be so. As for myself, I detested the imprisoned hours I spent mentally rearranging the panes in the stained-glass window, suggestive of the Victorian Gothic style which had remotely influenced the design, taken no doubt, from some builder's catalogue.

I could never make those little panes come right, alter them about as I would, or the arches and the pillars and the roof-vaulting, among which my mind busily wandered seeking for beauty and symmetry and finding none. I only knew that in the little simple stone kirk at Bavington I had been happier, and the shapes had been right; I was half a lifetime from knowing that its simple proportions were of the eighteenth century, to which architectural rightness came as naturally as wrongness to my own.

The congregation of shopkeepers and commercial travellers were no more my father's kind than they were of my mother's. He missed the warmth of that Methodism Coleridge so well described as 'a stove' ('heat without light', as he said); the revival meetings, the 'speaking with tongues', the 'simple faith'; but this he would never quite admit, for he, too, was trying to keep faith with a vanished past, though one neither my mother nor myself could share with him. He was a 'local preacher', as it was called; and I heard him preach to these people very often, in his beautiful calm voice. On week-nights too he often spoke for the League of Nations Union, which he saw as a practical means of leading the world a little nearer to that heavenly city which was, he believed, already coming down from heaven as an earthly reality as the socialist cause grew in power and numbers. The brotherhood of man of which the Gospel speaks he understood as an egalitarianism based on the abolition of property, a having of 'all things in common', like the first Christians. Communism, to him, was 'true Christianity', about to be realized at last in this world. I remember, soon after the war, his delight when Ramsay MacDonald's socialist government was returned to power. The kingdom seemed to him very near in which all these abstractions, universal brotherhood, peace between the nations, holding of all things in common, and so forth, were to be realized. The sermon I remember most clearly of all I heard him give —for even I was moved by his quiet certainty—was upon

111

that *civitas dei* which Plato saw, and St. John on Patmos, and St. Augustine and AE and many more, 'the holy Jerusalem descending out of heaven from God'. When my father spoke of that city it was impossible not to believe that many now living would see its walls of jasper, and sapphire, and chalcedony. My father was a pacifist, too; to kill was clearly, and under all circumstances wrong; therefore, war must be so. All his convictions, so calmly certain, were based upon rational over-simplifications of this kind; but for my mother and myself, these were not issues which ever arose; caught in the toils of life, we found no comfort in the generalized solutions of problems which were so remote from any that presented themselves to us. Yet among the precipices of her dreams my mother walked sure-footed; contrary to appearances, hers was a courageous soul caught in the toils; while my father's certainties were those of a natural timidity at home within the secure protection of the Christian virtues he practised and proclaimed. Non-conformist Christianity suited his nature; it did not suit my mother's; her nature craved for wilder, stranger, more beautiful myths. Neither she nor I had any wish to live in my father's ideal society. We would have found it as unendurably boring as the Cranbrook Park Wesleyan Methodist church itself.

My father, who had learned pure English only at Durham University and as a foreign speech, spoke it most beautifully. His father's household was, so to say, bilingual; the almost incomprehensible Durham dialect, the speech of childhood and freedom; educated English that of his later life. He had a fine ear both for speech and for music, and a knowledge both of the roots and meanings of words. From him I too learned to speak educated English, relinquishing my Border dialect, in which I had found a kind of freedom from constraint, a naturalness I have never since quite recaptured in the use of language. Between us and the surrounding barbarism of Ilford language was our protecting barrier. My mother's inheritance, her Scotch tongue; my father's

112

command, won by study, of the language (and with the words, the thoughts) of Chaucer and Shakespeare, Milton and Coleridge, Wordsworth and Emerson, Shelley, Browning, Tennyson (let me add, lest he should be misjudged, that he detested Dickens; 'a caricaturist', he called him, a vulgarian) and George Bernard Shaw. My father was a good linguist, and knew well both Latin and Anglo-Saxon, which for the sake of Bede, Cuthbert and Durham Cathedral, he loved especially; it was, for him, the speech of his ancestors, both natural and spiritual; his own, not a foreign, speech. In European languages and literature (other than Latin) he had little interest; preacher as he was of 'universal brotherhood' my father was by nature a xenophobe so complete that he was quite unaware of it; the Scotch, the Welsh and the Irish (not to mention the French) he regarded as a matter of course as alien and inferior. As for remoter races—negroes, Indians and Chinese—these had only a theoretical existence, 'on the mission field'; none of us had met any member of these exotic tribes.

Literacy set us apart, and gave us a sense—perfectly justified, so far as it went—of superiority to those who lacked it, even when, as was often the case, these were materially richer than ourselves; a kind of social isolation characteristic, I dare say, of schoolmasters' families. Poverty never troubled my father at all; he really had no desire for anything this world could offer; not even freedom, for he had that, also, in Heaven. Poverty was not my mother's problem, either (nor mine) but social displacement; many of the people of Bavington were poorer than the people of Ilford (or if rich, without living a kind of life essentially different from that of their poorer neighbours, tenant-farmer or hinds) but their way of life was one in which I could have been happy. My father gave me, instead, books; and with books, access to inner vistas, to the 'realms of gold'. But—this he did not realize—he was all the time, by placing in my hands the means of knowledge of ways of life

113

and thought other than any accessible to me, unfitting me for Ilford, sowing the seeds of unrest, of great unhappiness; for I was developing the ways of thought and modes of feeling of people who had lived in worlds where fine sensibilities were sheltered in walled gardens, and high thoughts in old libraries; where imagination led naturally to action in terms of existing possibilities. Shakespeare may be a fine education for a ruling class, but in the suburbs to think Shakespeare's thoughts is to be filled with energies, desires, impulses, which because they can have no outlets, no expression in the real, generate only fantasies and discontent. It was well I did not then know how far removed I was from those worlds which had created the poetry I fed upon, how many ranges of hills remained to be crossed, or I might have despaired of escape, which seemed to me then an easy matter. I did not know then how small a part of true culture book-learning is. During these years education rather replaced life than enabled me to live it; and the habit then formed, from which I have never since been quite free, of confusing things learned from books with lived experience. Yet where else but in the thoughts of others could I then have lived? Again I realize that, in my flight from a meagre reality into a world of extraneous knowledge, how typical I was of that very class I hated and despised.

Yet not everything in my mental world was of this extraneous kind; not poetry, not Shakespeare; these were as myself, were my life. I resented the intrusion into this world (mine by right of nature, as I felt), of school 'lessons', given by, and shared with, people who did not belong to the world of poetry at all. My unease in the academic world, and with people who have an immense amount, perhaps, of academic knowledge of 'English Literature' (and theirs with me, and with poets in general) is of this same kind: their knowledge is of this extraneous kind, and, however great, is not the same thing at all as the poet's knowledge of poetry; or, for that matter, that of the illiterate country people who found in the songs they learned, as I did, in their grandmothers' kitchens, the expression of their own, albeit collective, identity.

When I was twelve or thirteen, with Rutland Boughton's opera *The Immortal Hour*, the Celtic renaissance penetrated the prison-houses of the suburbs. People went to hear it ten and twenty times. When I heard it, in my turn, it was as if those summoning voices spoke to me. I knew who they were: 'How beautiful they are, the lordly ones, who dwell in the hills, in the hollow hills'. My people were not of this world—and with all my young and naïve soul in it I sang over and over to myself 'I will go back to the country of the young, and see again the faces of the Sidhe'. I thought these words held a secret meaning for myself alone; yet there must have been multitudes who, like me, heard those voices summoning back to a lost country. I did not then know that in Fiona Macleod's libretto there was transmitted a faint but authentic echo of a tradition as ancient as Pythagoras, known to Abaris, priest of the Hyperborean Apollo, who travelled on his golden arrow from those western isles which lay somewhere beyond the mean shops and proliferating human wilderness that blotted out the sunset fire from our windows. I did not see in those habitations of the lost yet another symbol of that human condition into which the souls (as Pythagoras taught, and the story of Eochaid embodies the same *gnosis*) 'descend'; the makers of myths had never looked so low; the Ilfords of this world seemed outside any mythological ordering principle which might give them even the dignity that belongs to the hells of traditional cosmogonies; a place and mode of being without symbolic orientation. Ilford had no part in the world of mythology or of a legend, was only its terrible negation; I was ashamed that I must return from Liverpool Street Station, where the world ended and the underworld began, to a place where the lordly ones could never find me, a habitation unvisited by the Gods.

For this I weep, and oft bewail my woe,
That e'er my soul such dreary realms should know.

Dispossessed as I was of my paradise I still clung, during
my school years, to its receding fringes. There were no
rivers or crags or burns any more; no longer even torpid
Essex lanes and misty fields and hedgerow elms. I turned
then to nature's minute worlds, and botany became a
passion. I entered those strange green labyrinths of interior
spaces, the cells and tissues of plants, and there my imagination found refuge in a world of form and beauty inviolate.
At Bavington I had climbed over the last dyke dividing the
human fields from the wild, setting foot on barren moor
and stony crag always with a sense of home-coming to the
sanctuary of wilderness immaculate. The human burden
dropped from me as I dropped over that frontier of rough
grey stones. There the wild in me came into its own, with
the curlews and the dry polypody fern in the clefts of the
rock; free. I entered that freedom as into a kind of ecstasy.
It was the same search for sanctuary which led me to
botany. My shrines now were those green inviolate spaces
of cell and vein, nucleus and astral body. These too were
wildernesses inaccessible to man, outside his narrow terri-
tory, untainted by his vulgarity, inaccessible to his stupid
destructiveness. Here no building estates could obliterate
the delicate order, the harmonious unfolding of living form.
In the little lighted circle of the microscope I was in the
great universe, not the small human suburb. The stars in
the great sky and the smallest particles bear a resemblance
often observed; as the sky extends into infinite spaces without, so the microscope is the way by which we may enter
spaces within, no less vast. Both are ways to freedom for
those who, as I did, feel their own world a prison-house.
For how many must science have been, as it was for me, an
escape into beauty! It is, besides, the escape most easily
accessible, even the only access of escape, precisely for the

children of the lower middle classes who have no access to any works of man which may be called beautiful; whose houses are mean and ill-proportioned, whose speech is ugly and inexpressive. Even the gramophone had scarcely yet begun, in those days, to make music available to the dispossessed; and 'wireless' was a primitive device with a piece of crystal and a short length of wire called a 'cat's whisker'. My father was interested in fiddling with this contraption, but I paid little attention to it beyond finding the piece of galena crystal rather beautiful.

The charm of science for me, at all events, was aesthetic; and perhaps metaphysical. The shapes of crystals, grown in saturated solutions of alum, copper-sulphate, potassium permanganate and the rest, each had its mysterious modular controlling its growth along line and plane. The behaviour of images in mirrors, where pins, viewed through lenses, reflected and refracted, multiplied and reversed themselves, appeared to be present where they were not, innumerable where there was but one, enlarged, diminished, transposed or made to vanish, first hinted that all may be illusion. The microscope too presented the living plant as a series of appearances—of worlds, one might say— among which that seen by the naked eye is but one we call more real than the others only from familiarity and because of the form of our organs of vision. Before I had heard of the *Vedas* I knew what is meant by Maya, the ever-fluctuating veil of appearances; I was a Berkeleyan before I knew who Berkeley was. I inhabited those marvellous minute worlds whose *magia* opened in the bright focus of the lenses of my microscope.

My grandfather had a set of green-bound volumes of natural history—(superficial enough, as I found to my disappointment when years later I came to look at them; written only for school teachers) which had, to my infant self, been works of pure magic. Each contained a construction like those which so delighted both Blake and Yeats in

William Law's Boehme, where 'you lift a flap of paper and see both the human entrails and the starry heavens'. Instead of Boehme's fires and demons, the Garden of Eden, the unregenerate heart and the Divine Name, there was a mollusc whose shell lifted to show first muscle, then viscera, then reproductive system; and a plant and a pigeon anatomy; not the supernatural causes underlying natural effects, but hidden anterior causes whose imaginative character was, to me, the same. These paper revelations had made something a little like what Boehme had meant clear to my infant eye: inexhaustible depth and strangeness and terror of byss and abyss. All things have, as it were—so those flaps of paper demonstrated well enough—only a thin surface in the visible world; and behind and beyond, mystery within mystery. And I wanted to know what lay at the heart of all.

Yet at every level of the real there is form; indeed—this I learned at the microscope which was, in those days, my most treasured possession—each world has its characteristic aspect, so that we may know, as it were, which forest we are walking in by its trees. The liquid shapes of cells; the network of nuclear structure, the geometry of foraminifera and radiolaria, of cylinder, spiral and cone; the rectilinear shapes of the inorganic, the curvilinear shapes of life; for the moist body, like the soul, seeks always to perfect itself as a sphere. Science is incommunicable in words; like music or painting it is a mode of knowledge in terms only of its own forms, which are non-verbal; natural forms, their relationships and transformations as such.

If, however, my musings over natural forms stirred in my imagination metaphysical apprehensions at variance with the fashionable materialism which claims 'science' as its ground, the remote marvels I beheld in the 'vegetable glass' did nothing to reconcile me with the Christian religion (in the debased form in which I knew it) which disregarded as it seemed to me, the beautifully ordered *gnosis* of a natural, without postulating any higher law, but merely the arbitrary 'Will of God', a person who, having made the universe, could 'prove' his existence only by arbitrary interventions; for such 'miracles' were supposed to be. Had I then known the Areopagite's celestial hierarchies, or the writings of Aquinas; if I had seriously read the Creeds, or discussed these with anyone possessing even the rudiments of a philosophic education I might have been less crude in my notions; but the scientists I read and met at that time were, unfortunately, far more intelligent than the Christians. I was for ever arguing my 'science' against my father's 'simple faith', unmoved by the figure of Jesus Christ, whose sublimity is self-evident to anyone who reads the Gospels with head unturned by the clap-trap of 'education' or perceptions undulled by some sentimental or stupid presentation. Truth to say whatever belonged to 'humanity' was for me, at that time and for long after, for that very reason suspect.

Had I learned Christianity from its art rather than in the pseudo-historical, pseudo-factual mode taught by non-conformists, I might have understood many things of which I had no conception until much later; until perhaps it was too late to make a Christian of me. But Christian art belongs part and parcel to Catholic Christendom; in the eyes of iconoclastic Protestantism, 'idolatry'. Failing to understand that art is the natural expression, as body to soul, the language of spiritual vision, those Protestant sects whose 'simplicity' (they were not really so simple; but their hymns and hymn-tunes and a certain sanctimonious use of language in extempore prayer they did not see, since these were not of 'wood and clay', as idols no less than the Madonna robed and crowned) was an expression of the illiteracy of the class amongst which they propagated themselves, had a horror of Catholic art. Such depictions as I saw at this time of the holy persons of the Christian story were sentimental trash manufactured for Sunday Schools and the mission field; and what they communicated—that effete meekness of the Sunday School Jesus—

119

revolted me. The persons and events of the Christian religion were, so my father insisted, unlike the Greek, the Celtic, the Egyptian, the Indian and all other mythologies, 'true'. Thus, not through my father's neglect but through his zeal I was thrown to the gods of the heathen; for if Christianity belonged to the world of fact, to 'real life', I wanted none of it: the truth I recognized was of quite another kind. The Greek gods (in whom I believed absolutely) were perfectly real because perfectly beautiful, and precisely insofar as they did not resemble 'real life' they possessed that perfection whose reality real life lacked. My early distaste for 'the Jesus of History', who was 'just like us' and who so unaccountably and surely mistakenly loved common men (the more ignorant the better, I was given to understand) has survived the subsequent conviction of reason that I had not understood, but misunderstood, the Christian vision.

I was, besides, given to understand that 'being good' was the essence of my Christian duty. Now I knew perfectly well that when I was 'being good' I was at my worst, like a child sitting still in a stiff chair. Pinned down to so narrow and negative a mode of being, compelled, besides, to pay attention to myself and to this 'being good' instead of to the marvels (whether of nature or of the imagination) which offered a world so much more spacious and more beautiful, I suffered, like my mother, from boredom, lack of interest in means and end alike; that 'good' Kathie who was the only outcome envisaged seemed to have nothing whatever in common with me, or with any of those great things I loved; rather that concentration of attention upon one's self seemed to close those vistas and expanses of nature and of poetry which were my real world.

But in the Greek gods (whose stories I found in my father's bookshelves where for him they formed part of 'the classics') I recognized the numinous principle which seemed to me to be entirely absent from my father's Christianity.

120

I became their secret worshipper, absorbing their stories with the same impassioned delight as I learned the orders of flowers. Not only or principally did I absorb these forms with their myths and divine attributes from simplifications and children's versions (*Tanglewood Tales* and *The Heroes*) but, especially, from Smith's Classical Dictionary, which it never occurred to me to find dull; on the contrary, because it contained knowledge for which I at that time craved, I found it absorbing. I recognized, in the simple enumerations of the divine attributes, as in the little line-drawings after gems and sarcophagi (in this respect also like the creatures of nature) essential meaning, intrinsically intelligible, and indescribable otherwise than in those very forms, acts, and symbolic attributes. Useless to tell me that the Sunday School Jesus was a figure to be venerated when from those depictions I was shown of Him I could see that this was not so. Intuition is of complex and subtle totalities, and recognizes wholes before it distinguishes their parts; therefore, simplified for children, the divine figures become not more but less accessible to the imagination of childhood. The soul, which recognizes the gods by what Plato calls anamnesis, the calling to mind of what is written in our nature, was never young and will never be old, but exists in another principle. Children well understand the language of expressive form, and the childish naïve is a sophisticated, adult and profoundly unimaginative taste. A child does not make critical comparisons, nor could I have said why I loved a dry-as-dust Classical Dictionary more than sentimental depictions and re-tellings 'for children' of the Christian story; but love itself is a judgement—the only judgement, after all, decisive in the end.

My increasingly inhuman 'scientific' vision had its dark side. At times 'objects' as we normally experience them seemed to lose their firm outline. How arbitrary, it then seemed to me, are those frontiers we choose to draw upon our world; we call this a table or a chair, that a rock or a lake, but what is that to nature? How precariously defined are the objects of our supposed knowledge, the picture of a world we paint upon the whirling shuddering flux of energy that plays before us. Sometimes the picture would disintegrate before my eyes, and all would be unknown and unknowable, without form and void; like so much painting of the present time which reflects that very experience of the dismantling and disintegration of the objects of the human world. Sometimes too I would look at people, seeing them not as people but as strange landscapes in which flowed rivers of blood where cells were living lives as separate as fish in an ocean from anything we call a 'person'. We look at a face and see it as wise, expressive, beautiful, human; but what is a face, looked at in terms of nature, matter, science, but a cluster of sense-organs gathered for convenience at the top of a spinal cord enlarged and convoluted into what we call a brain? What is it that makes a face a face, more than the chest or the belly, inexpressive and animal? So I would think; and upon the thought would follow the terrible shift of consciousness by which the human image was removed entirely, and I cut off from my kind in a material order uninformed by soul.

Yet my chemistry master it was who first showed me the one face which, even at that time, inscribed itself upon my knowledge in a manner not to be gainsaid; as if, after all, divine foreknowledge had prepared, in terms of those lowest of all 'facts' which convince scientists, a miracle they could not refute. The little booklet on the Holy Shroud he lent me described, if I rightly remember, the chemistry of it; a number of 'scientific' facts about how a linen cloth soaked in aloes and the like, and laid over a human body still warm, a body which had suffered the agony of extreme suffering, might undergo the chemical changes necessary to produce something like a photographic negative. What forger, in the early middle-ages or at some earlier time (the shroud had belonged to the House of Savoy, and its history has long

122

been known) would have thought of forging a negative image before the notion of a photographic negative existed anywhere in the world? But, of course, the scientists have their answers: there is nothing miraculous about the shroud, it is a mere matter of chemistry; what if it did once enfold the body of a man who was crucified, on whose brow are the marks of thorns and the spear-wound in his side? But that is not the miracle: the miracle is the face itself; *in imaginem dei*. The solemnity, the nobility, the peace, the perfect intellectuality and serene dignity of that face, of the tall kingly body, the folded hands, answered my folly, reproached my vanity, and kindled in my consciousness something like awe, recognition of the human mystery; for a face is something altogether other than the clay which bears its imprint.

CHAPTER THREE

A Suburban Idyll

I REVIVE the story of my thirteen-year-old self as if that
Kathie, who still wore her light-brown hair hanging
loose down her back on Sundays, had never been myself
at all; and perhaps she really never was, or only in a certain
sense. It is not that I wish to disown her—on the contrary,
her story is not without poetry, is perhaps like an old poem
found in a drawer and just good enough not to throw away;
but I can no longer evoke her as myself, as I can the Kathie
of Bavington. She was at best an aspect, not, like that earlier
child, the whole of what I was. How seldom indeed does the
whole person live and enact the present. However, if I was
not wholly present, neither was I, as at later and worse
times, wholly absent either.

The story begins by my father's bedside in the new local
hospital where he was lying with his leg in plaster; he had
been knocked off his bicycle by a tram in Ley Street. I was
visiting him on my way home from school at four o'clock;
his school-girl daughter, wearing her navy-blue drill-dress
over a fairly white blouse, and panama hat encircled with the
maroon and white school ribbon and badge; my two plaits
of hair wispy and bedraggled at the end of a school day. On
this day I found with my father a very tall young man with
a bony but pimpled face, green eyes, and strange lips, the
upper and the lower the same thickness, two long rectangles
meeting in a straight line which was curiously expressive.
To say exactly of what that line, well-drawn as by an artist,
was expressive, I find extremely difficult; I can evoke the

expression, but how put into words that characteristic fastidious look of discrimination, scorn, a sense of form and finesse which are seldom seen on faces in Ilford. That mouth proclaimed a non-participation more positive than reserve; yet the withdrawal was less a personal vanity than an aestheticism at odds with the world; Coriolanus' words to the common cry of curs whose breath he hated, unspoken but not unthought, might have drawn that line's 'I banish you'. This young man—to me he seemed a man—wore his well-cut suit with an air of natural elegance which made up for the pimples. Years later, seeing a portrait of Aubrey Beardsley, I recognized the type to which, both by nature and by imitation, he conformed. He looked like Beardsley; for in the suburbs people only look 'like' some person; the suburbs do not possess originals.

Roland Haye—he had recently added, like Balzac, a particle to his name in the hope of acquiring a little more identity and called himself, to the annoyance of his father, 'de la Haye'—had made some real effort to acquire the mental as well as the physical style of Beardsley, who for him was the type and exemplar of the culture to which he wished to become assimilated. This was the young man who, on my arrival, took his leave with a rather over-elaborate politeness, putting on his bowler hat with deliberate artistry. It was polite and perhaps thoughtful of Roland to have gone to visit my father, who had been his schoolmaster, and who also taught the young men's class at the Cranbrook Park Wesleyan Methodist Church, which Roland's family attended; but I do not think my father liked him, any more than he would have liked Beardsley himself as a visitor. The standards implied by Roland Haye's conscious artistry of dress and manner were no less suspect to him than those green eyes, more proper to goats than to sheep. Yet it was through his devotion to my father that I met the man who destroyed for ever the family life which until then had seemed immutable.

I loved my father, at that time, completely and uncritically. Perhaps, as the best of fathers are, he was a little in love with his beautiful daughter, his only child; a child in whose features he could see himself imaged in my mother's finer substance; a love at once narcissistic and blameless, his only happy love, perhaps. At that fatal meeting—for so it proved—I was entirely without foreknowledge. As for Roland, I must have noticed him, for I can see him clearly, in my mind's eye, more than fifty years after; but if intuition said anything at all, it did not say 'This man is your true love'; nor was he, for first and last he remained a stranger to my soul. There was no recognition of a fatal encounter, none at all, scarcely even a shudder at those repulsive pimples; and I wonder whether the long succeeding story of our first love, so poignant, so enchanting, was not, for me at all events, only a long irrelevance, a detour.

To what does free-will really amount at such times as the gods of life choose to cast us for some part in the immortal play but freedom to say Yes or No to the adventure of our destiny? Once we have said Yes there is little we can do, and the president of the Immortals, in Aeschylean phrase. . . . Ah well, I was not Tess, though my imagination at that time had certainly been formed by Hardy. It seemed to me then as if Hardy had written especially for me, that no one could understand, as I understood, passions natural and enduring, whole and unbroken, rooted in the earth itself. The gods may play with Hardy's people as they never could with James's or Proust's, subtle complex conscious beings as these may be, but the less plastic to the great opposeless wills. So at fourteen I was like one of those simple, deep-feeling unreflecting archetypal people who respond totally to the cosmic forces; but the other actors in the play acted from other scripts, or scriptures.

I find it extremely difficult to make a start on the narrative, to bring myself to look at those old photographs stored in my natural memory, but of which my soul has no memory at all. Could I, at the time, ever have believed it possible, that I would turn back so coldly to those once burning images? Yet I can see, written in the record of my life, that Book of Judgment, Roland (my father was home again now) coming through our garden gate, wearing this time (for it was Sunday) a blazer and an elegant straw boater. Elegance my father despised (as in P. G. Wodehouse, or Noël Coward) in part because all those loose locks, long locks, lovelocks, gay gear and going gallant the less Puritanical Gerard Manley Hopkins loved, reminded him, painfully perhaps, of those possibilities of myriadfold life from which the industrial poor must avert their eyes if they are to bear their lot. Those who live, besides, only to be, or to do, good, need (he no doubt would have thought) no elegance.

Was Roland's polite call made, this time, simply and solely on my father? It might have been so, for Roland had in him a deep need for a master whom he could admire and love. He played a little, as I remember, on that hated walnut piano, covered with silver vases and framed photographs, to which my mother drove me so unwillingly to 'practise', tearing me from my books. To my mother Roland appeared as an ally in her continual battle with her disobedient and ungrateful little girl, on whom money was spent which she could ill afford, to give me a 'chance' she never had, of acquiring the one useless accomplishment regarded, in that world, as desirable in a woman, to play the piano. Roland's example might help; he could play really difficult 'pieces', Ravel and Debussy and Chopin; if I would only practise, might not her child too be able to produce those dazzling allegros? In my home education was held to be able to produce anything and everything; heredity was discounted. Heredity was I think obscurely felt to be 'unfair', whereas education gave everyone a 'chance'. My mother was, besides, blind to the fact that I had inherited, not her own exquisitely soft hands with their touch of fairy delicacy, but my father's strong fists with knotted joints; the heritage of

127

generations of coal-miners, the tools of whose craft were the pick and the shovel. When it was that Roland's green Cornish eyes first fell upon me I do not know; but soon after that call, our little family of three people whose lives seemed as one was electrified by an event unprecedented: Roland called to ask if I might go to tea at his house the following Sunday; he would call for me and return me to my parents at the evening chapel service.

I was perhaps flattered at being singled out, but, even more, enchanted by the vista I glimpsed opening from the boredom, the non-life which so long had held me. I saw a path and wanted (of course), to follow it and to see to what marvels it might lead. Certainly love was a thought which never crossed my mind; but thoughts of music, books, and a wonderful young man who knew so much of these things seemed something altogether to be desired. My mother, as innocent as myself, never dreaming that her little girl (for I was still, even physically, a child) could attract a young man who played Chopin and talked of Frazer's *Golden Bough* (not a book known to my father, since it had appeared after his student-days and was not on the school syllabus) otherwise than intellectually, backed me up; nor did I see any reason why my father should not approve of an acquaintance so educational. It was a shock to me when he was angry and troubled, as though I had suggested doing something wrong. Conscious of my innocence, thinking him unjust, I argued and protested like the spoiled child I was; for my parents had always told me that children should be given a reason for obedience, not merely asked to obey. Did not, I argued, the Hayes go to the Cranbrook Park Wesleyan Methodist Church? Were they not, therefore, good people? Why did he not like Roland? And so, against his judgement, my father gave in. It was my first serious disobedience; and even to this day I do not know who was right, my father, acting as he did from his experience, or I, winged with the impulse of life.

Had I obeyed, had I at every stage obeyed my father, I would never, certainly, have become a poet. I would have become, had he had his wish, I suppose, first an English mistress in a good girls' secondary school, and perhaps in the end a headmistress. I would have lived a life of social usefulness, a life dedicated to the service of 'others', my happiness in religion, my relaxation singing, perhaps, in some church choir. I do not think that at any point in my father's ambitions for me marriage would have been thought of; I do not think he had any illusions about marriage; he had seen too much of those weary slaves who

> With one chained friend, perhaps a jealous foe
> The dreariest and the longest journey go.

His own marriage to my mother he would have said was an exceptionally happy one; it would have been worse than useless to think otherwise. He would, I think, have wished me to avoid, if possible, a pitfall which at worst could open into a hell, and at best could lead to—well, not to what the poets have called love.

My mother, for her part, wished me above all to be 'pretty' and happy and to be able to accompany songs on the piano; not to ruin my eyesight over books, but to have 'a husband and children' as was 'natural' for 'young girls'. All these in the abstract, or collective sense. That, on one level; that is what she would have said she wished for me because she knew that 'mothers' (the general term again) did wish just that for their 'daughters'. She very often reproached me for not being like 'other daughters'; but then, was she like 'other mothers'? She would never have confessed, even to herself, the wild aberrances of her true dreams and desires; but I believe that, secretly, she wanted me to live out the myth, to walk with the gods, to explore those long vistas of passions, and dreams and intellections, forbidden to her. I wonder, now, if my life has not been a realization of my mother's most secret dreams. It was she who wrote down, before I could hold a pencil, those first poems so many children make; she, not my father, English master as he was, who treasured my words in her heart.

No doubt my father was right in his sense that the *dharma* of a schoolmaster's daughter was to be a schoolmistress not a poet. He had a strong sense of social order, never realizing that my mother and I had never in fact belonged to the world he served; we were social exiles, no terra firma under our feet, able only to sink or to soar in a great void. This was self-evident to her and to me; but he never knew that in marrying my mother he had married a being of another element. Her seal-skin hidden in the domestic meal chest she never found; never returned to the ocean of her freedom. It was I who found it, I who was set free.

When I overruled my father, and, abetted by my mother, went to tea with Roland, I was at the first parting of the ways. Now, still suffering as I am from the lifelong consequences, still permanently injured from the many wounds I received, and still more by those I gave, because of what followed, I try to remember again what made me choose; what, indeed, I did choose. It was not, certainly, sexual desire, or even sexual vanity. My choice had nothing to do with sex at all. Roland offered, as I immediately sensed, a culture less meagre than that of my home; the living culture of our time, Gilbert Murray and Frazer, Jane Harrison and the Celtic Revival, Flecker and Dowson and the Testament of Beauty and Promenade concerts, instead of home, homework and Methodism.

But if I chose rightly the choice had its price; never was the breach between my father and myself quite mended. I rejected, then, his dearest values; and among the gods who judge, if some cast white stones for me, others cast black, and rightly so. I rejected socialism and the greatest good of the greatest number for those values which few can reach, in the belief that the high and beautiful things are of value in themselves; are the true ends of life, which the breeding generations exist only to serve and to realize. I think I already knew all that at the time very clearly. I rejected 'whatsoever thy hand findeth to do . . .' as a principle that can lead to a static and narrow virtue. My mother and I had seen vistas of wonder, the green green ways to fairyland. My mother only saw those vistas; I travelled them. The scale fell as it was loaded, on my mother's side. It was my mother in me who before me had walked on the heather moors, who was always watching for a door to open. What I would find through the door mattered little; there was a door and through it I went on my way, or perhaps my Way.

So I went to tea with Roland Haye on the following Sunday. He arrived to call for me, and we walked, in embarrassed silence, along misty muddy Essex lanes and along by the wooden fence of the Claybury asylum, through a bluebell wood, and so back into suburbia and privet hedges to the Hayes' house; 210 Cranbrook Road; a house in the 'better', and older, part of Ilford, a house with some rudiments of refinement, and maid in cap and apron to open the front door.

Roland and I had in common one passion: our hatred of suburbia, our determination to escape. He like me was in exile. Old Mr. Haye was a Cornishman, from Hale, a grey squirrel in a London office who had never become tamed to his cage; he too loved Hardy's novels with that passion we feel only for works that tell our own story. Hardy held before old Mr. Haye images of that from which he was so bitterly exiled, a life still unsevered from its ancient roots. Mrs. Haye too was an exile, but of another kind; each suffered alone. She had met her true love after the birth of her first child, Roland; whom, in consequence, she never perhaps loved. He, the lover in the world of never-to-be, was I think a doctor; for a large print of *The Doctor* hung on a wall of the living room. Now she was houseproud, her dark oak furniture (replica Jacobean) gleamed and her cakes never failed to rise; yet no one in the house was happy.

131

Those Sunday visits became habitual. Roland would take me into the little dining-room at the back of the house, where he would sit down at his upright piano, piled high with music. There I would sit beside him on a dining-room chair, and he played Chopin's Nocturnes and Mazurkas and his Ballades, whose language of wild longing spoke for Roland's soul, as Hardy's less passionate nostalgia for his father's; Chopin and Ravel and Debussy. He made me sing, to his accompaniment, the Kennedy Frasers' adaptations of Hebridean songs; the first echo of the Celtic revival to reach me. Afterwards we would walk to the church where I would rejoin my parents in their pew.

Roland was already at cross-purposes with the Methodists, amongst whom he regarded my father as a shining exception. The culture which made my father suspicious of Roland from the beginning was of course bound to make Methodism intolerable to him; 'a veneer of culture', my father contemptuously called it; but what else, after all, could it be, in that world? Roland was bound to the Cranbrook Park church only by being the assistant organist, sitting in the organ loft turning the pages for Mr. Raymond Causer. To have access to an organ was, after all, something; but he had already begun to struggle against the crassness, vulgarity and stupidity of a religion of shopkeepers. Mr. Haye, like my father, was loyal to a Methodism which no longer existed, the revivalism of John Wesley who had preached, bare-headed, to the rough and ignorant men of the Cornish tin-mines as he had preached to the coal-miners of County Durham. Both were for ever deploring the falling-away of Methodism from that early fervour, but without learning the obvious lesson from history.

I cannot suppose that in the silent, light-brown-haired school-girl Roland had divined a kindred rebel. I do not suppose he wished me to have any attributes but those of the mirror of his dreams and longings. I, for him, was to be that which Chopin so mournfully and exquisitely desired,

132

the for-ever-unattainable soul of love. For him I was virginity itself, that infinite potentiality upon which he might project passions erotic and religious at once.

It is false to imagine that 'love' can be considered as something distinct from a culture. The mere animal instinct is less than human unless tinged with some mode of feeling, shone upon by the light of imagination, adorned in some style, humanized and ordered by poetry or music. Our style was the nostalgia of Chopin; nostalgia for a perfection high beyond hope of attainment, for which we would rather live in mourning for ever than once forget. The religious eroticism of Verlaine; 'And behold, a Virgin shall conceive and bear a child' overwhelmed us with its archetypal power in a way almost impossible to convey to those for whom mere carnality had dulled the resonances of the awe-inspiring mystery of the incarnation which lies behind sexual desire, the mournful ecstasy of Rossetti's lovers who with burning eyes gaze upon one another in a still trance that possession itself would break. How precariously such love hung suspended over the sorrowful depths of the Decadence I had not read enough of the literature of the time to know; Roland certainly was haunted by some shadow of Dorian Gray, and of 'that wicked book' (a very childish book, but then we were children and Huysmans the acme of sophistication to Roland). Yet our love was not without forms and images which gave to it the semblance of a style which we, struggling to rise above an environment devoid of culture, and above all devoid of style, strove with a certain heroism to create. It is true that we dressed our passion in the masks created by others; but for what are the forms of art created unless to enable the *filii et filiae* to live their loves beautifully?

For, before many Sundays had passed, we had been assigned by the immortals the parts they had all along known we would play. I remember the failing afternoon light shining, as in a Rossetti painting, through the west window into the little crowded room. We had not gone

133

with the family to church but remained alone in the house, with the maid. Roland played, and I turned the pages of his music. Perhaps he played only moderately well, but the music spoke to us all its message of Paradise, of a time and a place where we were not but longed to be, as we sat caged in the little suburban back room, our narrow view closed, beyond the William Morris curtains, by Mr. Haye's mown lawn and his chrysanthemum plants tied stiffly to their bamboo canes. We yearned for what Chopin yearned for, but possessed no more than we.

He played the third Ballade; and, like Dante's lovers—Roland must have known them, if only through Rossetti, though I did not—we were entranced by the beauty of what we had heard; or rather, Roland was, for in retrospect I can see that I am telling his story, not my own. His left hand, leaving the keys, he laid on my right hand; his narrow hand, with its 'tied' thumb. I was afraid, though of what I did not know. He could scarcely speak as he asked me to go with him into the front parlour; the room where *The Doctor* hung. He led me to his father's big leather arm-chair, and there he seated me, as on a throne; then with deliberation (how often had he, in fancy, rehearsed this scene?) he placed a brown velvet cushion on the carpet at my feet, and kneeling on it he declared his love; a boy's first love, for the archetypal virgin. He would wait, he said, for five years, for seven years; no matter for how long: 'some day you will be my wife', he said. Someday, someday, that infinite distance between desire and realization which passion peoples with images of the beautiful, with poetry, music and painting; for the distance between a dream and a realization is greater than we knew: nothing less than the distance between Plotinus' here and yonder: a distance in kind. Does not all the poetry of life lie in that enchanted land between our desire and its goal?

I had no thought of love; certainly none for Roland. If in my imagination a lover lay hidden it was not he. That, as I

134

sat enthroned in the Sunday evening fading glow I very well knew; indeed I was about to say so, but was too surprised and too embarrassed to find words. I was a child absolutely, a virgin as ignorant as Verlaine himself could have wished. But before I had found those words for which I searched, Roland had said, 'May I kiss you?—only one kiss', and those lips of equal width had touched mine before the shudder of revulsion from the pimples, the bony jaw, the green eyes of the wrong man could form itself into words of refusal. So he kissed my lips, and from one moment to the next I ceased to be a child and knew instantaneously that I was a virgin destined for the wedding night.

As he had placed that brown cushion so deliberately at my feet, I had realized, with odd clarity, that the scene was rehearsed. But after that kiss, he repeated the lines (were they too rehearsed?)

> O lyric Love, half angel and half bird
> And all a wonder and a wild desire—

—and I was taken and caught. It seemed as though the lines were given to me as faith is plighted with a ring of gold. So our particular selves respond to the universal of the ever repeated story, each saying, in Yeats's words, 'Oh that none ever loved but you and I!' The words were as if spoken by Roland to me alone; the living test of true poetry.

To say I loved Roland at that moment would be untrue; I never loved him, perhaps never even liked him. But he awoke in me 'love', impersonal erotic love, and laid claim to it before I could draw breath to refuse; and since he it was who had evoked in me that virgin passion, I could no more escape than the *kore* from Pluto's gloomy palace; indeed I felt myself to be bound by a solemn, sacramental bond to him, a man whom I would not have chosen, did not choose.

Perhaps in a simpler age that great inflowing tide of instinctive life on which we were so ecstatically swept away would have been enough to carry the *filii et filiae* through the

135

stations of puberty and marriage and the bearing of children, upborne on the single long green wave of the life, impersonal and immortal, that lives in us. In Arcadia, youth and maiden are interchangeable, the individual mattering only insofar as he and she can play the parts assigned, embody the genius of the one life; and participation in that impersonal wave of life and all its deep joy and wisdom, which informs now one, now another young and nubile body, is the reward of obedience to the great opposeless wills. I can see why, since natural love is such, marriages may be called indissoluble; if the mystery goes by the pattern there can be but one initiation, and the virgin is bound for ever to the man who with a kiss summons her to the play.

Neither then nor later did Roland attempt to seduce me— the *mores* of our class and generation precluded that no less than did the poem we were living, the music we echoed. Yet in that ill-starred first love I knew and understood all that the mere gods have to reveal, an instantaneous epiphany of the mysteries of womanhood. How awe-inspiring, how sacred it all seemed, as if I had passed through some initiation, as if the parlour in Cranbrook Road had been some *villa dei mysterii*, and *The Doctor* that bull-faced Dionysus whose phallic power makes the little brown-haired virgin weep on the knees of the priestess: but I had no priestess to advise or comfort me: all must be kept secret, for what would our parents say? They must not know.

So we set out upon our seven years' waiting. The wedding night was for us to be the realization of the perfection of all the joy, beauty and freedom of which works of art are but a reflection; so we thought. But had we known it, only another symbol of that for which the soul waits, another reflection as 'mirror in mirror mirrored is all the show'. But we never travelled far enough to learn that; the memory of first love remains for ever captured in the amber light of Rossetti's *Beata Beatrice*, the resonance of the third Ballade of Chopin.

136

But if the two goddesses did not, after all, get my virginity, they exerted all their power to claim what was their due; as, being goddesses, precisely, of the life-cycle, they are bound to do. On those Sunday walks along the asylum fence, Roland's long bony arm would now be round my waist; and in the little wood we would kiss beneath a wild apple-tree and weave dreams of that 'someday'. We would spend the first night of a bliss never-to-be in some Greek temple built in Avalon among the apple-trees, the singing and the gold; or we would change the style and live in a small brown house built for love and us to dwell in, in a forsaken garden where now sleeps the crimson petal now the white, and the rose-red seaweed mocks the rose. The golden world lay, for Roland, west of Cornwall, where sweet gales blew and the pebbles on the strand were all of amethyst. We were much indebted not only to *art nouveau* but also to the Celtic revival for the adornments of our dream house under its *ciel féerique et divin*; or, again, ought I to say that he was; and I, ignorant enough, naïve enough, amorous enough, young enough to follow enthralled, trod on his dreams; softly, I hope.

With all this he told me, with much emotion, the facts of sex, exacting a promise that I would bear his child; and I, powerless as a rabbit before a weasel, or like Milton's lady in the chair of another enchanter, had not the power to refuse, though my blood ran cold at the thought, for I did not want any child at all, and certainly not his. The *ciel féerique et divin* was another matter; that I did not see merely as nature's ruse to cheat us into fulfilling her ends. Even then, was I planning in my heart to cheat nature for the sake of poetry?

For although I gave myself so completely to the weaving of a dream, something in me remained aloof. Meanwhile I was content to be the mirror of his dreams, which passed over the surface of my fancy without leaving a trace. Beneath its surface I still kept secret faith with my intention of becoming a poet; the two futures were both too remote for their incompatibility to become a reality to be reckoned with.

And yet in retrospect I realize what golden doors he opened. He took me, on his nineteenth birthday, to the Queen's Hall, to hear Casals play the Bach 'cello suite; my first concert. Afterwards we went to an Italian restaurant in Charlotte Street (among so many I have never found it again)—my first Italian restaurant. With our meal we drank cider; my first alcohol, amber essence of the apple tree, the singing and the gold. It was with Roland I saw *The Immortal Hour*, with Gwen Ffrangçon-Davies in the part which enchanted my generation. He gave me, on my birthday, a bottle of scent; my first scent, *Tréfle Incarnat*, blown over summer meadows filled with dewy clover. My father, who dearly loved the theatre, had taken me to Shakespeare, to Ibsen, to Galsworthy, to Barrie, to Shaw; I had loved these happy family occasions, but they had not the magic of first love in them; and Roland, besides, was of my generation, and we listened—or he listened and I echoed what he heard —for the new voices that spoke for our time. Never were two star-crossed lovers more athirst for poetry and music which would give us the words and melodies in which our great love could be clothed in forms of beauty worthy of it. If we consumed much bad poetry, we at least kept our souls alive on it.

It was Roland who first quoted Blake to me; the Blake beyond *Songs of Innocence*, that is. He had, I think, read Swin-burne's essay on Blake (Swinburne's dead roses and the rose-red seaweed that mocks the rose flourished in the coign of a cliff in our Western paradise, and his asterisks stirred in us strange emotions, for even asterisks can be incitements to carnal desires) and believed, like Swinburne, that Blake was on the side of 'evil'; as, by our parents' standards, so he was. I was much appalled by some of the Proverbs of Hell, with their incitement to a carnality which I knew was, when all was said and done, forbidden fruit.

We would both surely have outgrown that first love; and now I wonder if Roland, as he murmured Dowson's lines,

My heart is sick of an old passion;
I have been faithful to thee, Cynara! in my fashion—

was not already aware of the long vista of a life in which our young love would be something long past. This love, into which he poured the very essence of his soul, and all the words and the music of immortality which he would make his own, he laid down, like wine, to mature perhaps when he was old. It was as if this love, so pure it was, could never again be equalled by anything his life could bring to flower; a love beautiful, sorrowful, renunciatory, a minor poem in the mode of the Décadence composed by a strange imaginative exile from a world of art who might, had he not been born in Ilford, have been an original and not a mere replica. When he quoted *Cynara* I too was moved by a strange mournful presentiment. In the moment of intensest life, in the very Now of Arcadia, we seemed almost to foreknow, with a poignancy of pity, the later selves we would be, who would have wandered away from the apple-tree, who would be far from the singing and the gold, the present ecstasy so intense that we could not conceive a state in which it would have been forgotten; and if we could, our grief for that forgetting would have been the stronger. So I remember my Arcadian self wept for what we might become; yet now the exile can look back upon those young lovers in their Arcadia without envy, indeed with another kind of pity, a pity without grief. 'The wind blows the ghosts out of the garden'; when together we read *Hassan* we did not know that we were ourselves the ghosts.

But the end, for us, involved more painful and more complex passions than those of the poems on which we fed our dreams.

I told my mother, as I remember, as we walked home

together one evening after my weekly piano lesson; Roland, I said, had asked me to marry him, and I had promised: in seven years' time. 'But you are only a bairn', she said. She in her innocence had no more imagined such a possibility than I had myself, and must now have reproached herself bitterly for over-persuading my father, who had proved to be right. I too had a guilty conscience; and so now I made her promise to keep our secret; and I think she did promise. But of course such a promise neither could nor should have been kept; and not long after, the storm broke. It was again a Sunday, as I remember, and I was playing hymns on my unloved piano, singing Wesley's 'Jesu lover of my soul' with the pleasing emotion of one who had never known the rolling of waters or the high tempest outside the words and music of the hymn itself. My parents were upstairs in their bedroom and I could hear them talking. Presently my mother came downstairs, much distressed and weeping; then my father; and the storm of life broke upon me then. He began to question me: what had Roland said, done? He had not seduced me, indeed; but he had kissed me; and he had touched my breast. Never before had I seen my father in a passion of anger, and my soul froze. He did not blame me, but only Roland, using of him words that seared my very soul by the ugliness and obscenity with which they suddenly defiled the texture of our dreams. He forbade me ever to see Roland again. My poor father left the house in grief and rage, saying he was going to kill Roland. I do not blame my father—he after all knew more of 'life' than I, and feared I would be, or had already been, seduced. His one miscalculation was the strength of his own moral influence, not only upon myself but upon Roland as well, who admired my father boundlessly. We were, besides, so young that we thought nothing of waiting five, ten, a thousand years for the realization of the shimmering dream; even, perhaps, it was the dream we wanted, not the realization; but how it might have ended if my father had not intervened it is useless to speculate. Unfortunately he intervened too late, and his prohibition served only to strengthen what we now thought of as our great love. What was worse was the searing by my father's indictment as something obscene of a love that had seemed too pure and beautiful for this earth. From that wound, as it seems to me fifty years later, I never quite recovered.

How long before was it, I wonder—I recall the dream suspended out of time, but it belonged, certainly, still to childhood—that I woke one night from one of my night-mares (I was subject to bloodcurdling nightmares, nearly all now forgotten) and cried out for help? How often had my father's calm and comforting presence driven away my demons! On this night, I saw my bedroom door open, and my father came in; but then his face changed and turned into a demon-face and I screamed again, this time in the very extreme of terror. This time my real father heard me, and came up the stairs, and comforted me; the first awaken-ing had been a dream within a dream. Now the nightmare seemed to enact itself in waking life.

I would not, even now, have for a moment considered disobeying my father; but Roland, whom he had visited and forbidden to see me, and I do not doubt scathed and seared, though of course without doing him any physical violence —for that would have been against his mild Christian code —did disobey; he wrote me a letter asking me to meet him: he would stand, he said, every Sunday at a certain gate into the fields and wait for me. But I gave my father the letter and did not go.

There was, however, one way we could, if not meet, at least see one another, which not even my father could forbid. The Hayes' pew in the Cranbrook Park Wesleyan Methodist Church was at right-angles to ours in the transept under the pulpit. Twice on Sundays and once on Wednesday evenings we could gaze at one another askance, Roland sitting beside his father and mother, sister and brother; and I, my light-brown hair loose on my shoulders under my blue velour hat, between my parents. Nor was it only to see my lover that I insisted on going to all the services, even the week-night evening services, but also, after the first shock of guilt and sorrow, in the hope of finding help in the religion in which my father himself so fervently believed; so mixed are our motives. Perhaps also I wanted to prove to my father, by carrying it into the bosom of his own chapel, the innocence of our great love.

I remember one November night—only a few weeks after our separation—a fog came down so thick that after the Wednesday evening prayer meeting I could scarcely see the road; and then, a little in front of me, I saw Roland, his tall stooping figure darkly wrapped in a grey greatcoat. He did not—faithful to our promise to my father, since I wished to obey—speak to me, but made a sign to me to follow him; and, Orpheus-like, he led his Euridice through the yellow fog, the light of his electric torch showing me the pavement. The nimbus of moisture on the texture of his greatcoat enshrouded him in foggy dew, like those souls who, descending into the Hades of this world become, so the mythologists tell, 'drenched in moisture'. He led me through the bye-roads of Ilford, and up Cranbrook Road to the garden gate of West View; and only then did he turn, looked at me in a farewell charged with all the nostalgia of the poetry we loved; and we parted, he like Clerk Saunders into a darkness where I might not follow him, I through the gap of the privet hedge, whose each leaf was edged with its rime of cold mist, to our front door where the dim light in the hall was broken into a pattern like a shattered star through the frosted glass of the pane. How clearly the images return, how far and faint the emotions of the actors! After this, I memorized at school the Shakespeare sonnet

Let me not to the marriage of true minds
Admit impediments; Love is not love
142

Which alters when it alteration finds,
Or bends with the remover to remove.

This too was an act of defiance against my father's authority, for Shakespeare, like John Wesley, could not be called in question; but I remember how savagely he said to me, 'very well, love in your minds as much as you like, I am only concerned that you do not meet again in the body'. I took up the challenge, and tried, poor child, poor stubborn wilful child, to learn Shakespeare's love of minds; for I did not doubt that Shakespeare and Wesley were at one with my father in their condemnation of the flesh; as perhaps they are.

Religion, then, was for us not so much a source of wisdom, strength or love, as a weapon; to me a defensive shield, but to Roland, more resourceful than I, also of attack. To Methodist fathers only one thing was perhaps worse, in those days, in their young than a love affair, and that was 'going to Rome'. Roland began to show signs of going to Rome.

The signs indeed had already begun to appear before our enforced separation. When I first saw the elegant pimpled youth with the boater, Roland was earning his living as a clerk in the Patents Office by day, and studying medicine at evening classes at King's College in the Strand. Perhaps he was fulfilling his mother's secret instigation, her old love for the nameless one in whose honour *The Doctor* hung in the parlour, whose heavy furniture she so dutifully and so joylessly polished. At about the time we met, Roland had passed his first M.B. examination; and now he must ask his father for the money to continue his studies as a full-time medical student.

No one, not even his mother, knew what his father's salary was; and when the old Cornishman refused, Roland assumed—his mother too, it may be—that his father could have, but would not, pay for his son's training. No one ever knew; but how precariously the respectability of suburban households was suspended over a chasm no one in Ilford could long forget. Only when the circuit-steward of the Cranbrook Park Wesleyan Methodist Church died behind his trim privet hedge was it discovered that months before he had lost his job, and that his widow had not enough money to buy a coffin. And so, one day, entering the office where for thirty years or more he had worked for a city firm of wholesale drapers, the little Cornishman was told that his services were no longer required. He was within a year of pensionable age, and this dishonourable form of economy was well known in the City. The class with whom such risks were taken could not retaliate, lacking the means, or indeed the mentality, to defend themselves; for the shame of letting it be known that they had been 'sacked'. Mr. Haye's story is a typical Ilford tragedy; the shock nearly killed him. But that was some years later.

Who, then, is ever to blame for anything? The father best knew his own insecurity; not a young man when he married he had two children younger than Roland; but the eldest son bitterly blamed his father for debarring him from his dream of becoming a doctor, not knowing over what a void was suspended that neat, restrictive suburban villa with trim maid in white cap and apron.

It was soon, then, after my first visit to the Hayes' house that Roland led me up to his room, pulled open the bottom drawer of his chest, and showed me in it his white overall, folded away. To it was pinned a card on which he had written the word 'forgotten'. This he made me read. How typical that childish histrionic gesture; but only now do I realize that the closing of the career upon which he had set his heart was more than a disappointment; it was a mutilation. His, too, was a typical suburban tragedy.

With medicine, forgotten or no, barred to him, Roland turned to religion; for the bars of Ilford chafed him more painfully than ever now that a way of escape had been closed. He quoted much from *The Hound of Heaven*; I never liked the poem, then or now, a hound pursuing a creature it would presently tear bleeding to pieces seeming to me now, as then, an image singularly inapt for the divine love; besides the inevitable confusion with *The Hound of the Baskervilles*. However, the poem served, for Roland, the double purpose of fitting his mood of religiosity, and of annoying his father. Since the author was a Catholic the plain implication was that Roland was being hounded into the Church of Rome. He began to sneer and jeer at 'Prots'; he would tell, in the same spirit of defiance as I memorized Shakespeare's one-hundred and sixteenth sonnet, the story of some evangelical called Kensit, deservedly killed by a brick heaved at him by an outraged Irish Catholic for 'insulting Our Lady'.

Rome, in Ilford, was known to those of us who had never crossed the forbidden threshold of the Catholic Church in the High Road in the person of Father Palmer; whose aged figure was to be seen in Ilford's older and drabber 'Streets' and 'Roads', and even sometimes in the newer 'Gardens' with their well-kept secrets. His flat, wide clerical hat suggested the alien and ancient faith he represented; nor was it entirely imagination that set him apart from the ministers and even the vicar, who were not 'priests'; a word that still carried, in my childhood, a dread significance, of the fires of the Inquisition. His lined face, as I recall its awful impact upon me, was like a relief-map of the human condition; disturbingly, frighteningly unlike the unwritten, unmade faces of the suburb-dwellers amongst whom we moved. And because I was too young to see it as beautiful the old priest's face seemed to me ugly. His presence amongst us was somehow alarming: 'There's Father Palmer', my mother would say, while he was still a long way off. And his passing would remind us that in our town still dwelt the Scarlet Woman. For Catholics, we knew (and we knew little else), worshipped the Virgin Mary, and were for the most part sinners. They 'went to confession' and were absolved of their sins by the priest, only to commit the very same sins again almost immediately afterwards. To me, brought up in a religion which imposed the simple obligation never to sin, this seemed very strange and shocking; for I had never consciously met any person who had 'sinned', but only 'good' people to whom it never occurred to think of themselves as sinners, or even as potential sinners. Therefore when Father Palmer passed, he brought with him the aura of his unholy holy office of ministering to that unknown, anathematized section of humanity, its sinners.

Just how true this picture was I learned nearly fifty years later, from one who had known Father Palmer better than I. Remembering Ilford and its dire respectability, what more natural than that conversation should turn also to Edith Thompson; who in her tragic story had so poignantly experienced the frustration that world of drab mediocrity imposed upon a dream of love and joy and beauty. She, a dreamer of those dreams which in Ilford belonged to the world of never-to-be, was convicted of the murder her lover committed for her sake. Dreaming a dream like hers, I attempted to make poetry its realization; and Roland— dreamed of becoming the anathematized thing itself and seeking Paradise in the habit of religion. So it was, that, fifty years after, I heard how Edith Thompson, condemned and waiting for her hanging (and how I too had waited with her through that interminable agony of delay) had wished to be received into the Catholic Church; for where else could she have hoped to find refuge? And she had sent for Father Palmer. The English law had not allowed her to receive instruction and baptism from him; for she was recorded in their books as 'C. of E.'; but he did visit and converse with her at the distance prison bars allowed; and after her death her sister had received the baptism Edith Thompson had only desired. There had been another murderer too—the 'taxi-cab' murderer, a young man who had committed a

146

crime of passion (his victim was a Catholic actress) and who, apalled at his own guilt, had likewise sent for Father Palmer. He, more fortunate than Edith Thompson, had been received into the one Refuge of Sinners that suburban Hades knew.

My father, like most of those we knew, had held the sentence upon Edith Thompson to be just; for she had been guilty of a crime only less pardonable than murder—adultery. Whatever might be said of forgiveness, the Puritan morality was in truth that of the Old Testament—'the wages of sin is death'; dread words early making my own heart contract with fear, for all my earnest resolve never to 'sin'. That morality knew nothing of 'sin' as a state of being; only of 'sins', discoverable, specific acts which were at all costs to be avoided. No sacramental forgiveness of sins mitigated that narrow and simple rule. The pity was less that some of its adherents were hypocrites than that so many practised that morality with total and life-destroying sincerity.

It was Roland who had told me that old story about the man who, having committed a murder, rushed in remorse to his Protestant Minister, only to be told never to set foot in chapel again. He then went to the Vicar, who was embarrassed by so ungentlemanly an avowal. He went last of all to the Catholic Priest, and brought out once more his confession, 'Father I have committed murder'. The reply, 'How many times, my son?' was not, for us, a joke; it was too close to the reality in which we were ourselves involved.

Therefore it was that when, in his turn, Roland found himself in the toils of life and accused by my father of 'sin', he too turned to the Church of the Virgin Mary, the Refuge of Sinners; though not to Father Palmer, for Roland's sense of style demanded some more dramatic, more aesthetic setting. It was to Westminster Cathedral of which another pupil of Father Palmer is now Cardinal Archbishop (accessible to him from his 'office' in the City) that he went seeking sanctuary.

147

Indeed that great building was a vital part of the whole aesthetic network of interwoven strands which made up the culture of those years. From Verlaine to Francis Thompson, from *A Rebours* to *La Cathédrale*, from *La Fille aux cheveux de lin* to *La Cathédrale Engloutie*, from the white overall to soutane and biretta was a modulation of key entirely within the style of the period. The brick walls of the cathedral were still austerely bare, but for the encrusted richness of a few chapels. Eric Gill's Stations of the Cross were new, and no less potent as symbolic embodiments of the aspirations of our age than the Sidhe, or Gilbert Murray's little green-backed volumes of Euripides, or Vaughan Williams's music, or Cecil Sharp's collections of folk-songs. What more natural to a youth hurt, frustrated in his ambition to become a doctor, his texture of love-dreams torn by the conflict of guilt, than to turn to that religion, more authoritative than parents, which can open even in the suburbs a door of escape from meanness of culture and narrowness of life into all the grandeur, beauty, dignity and wisdom of Christian civilization? Perhaps, too, like Poe, Thompson, Huysmans and the rest, there was something of the erotic-sensuous in the spell which drew him to the dull gold of dim mosaic, the wavering candles, the still sanctuary-lamp in dark side-chapel, and that great Byzantine cross which hangs suspended in the incense smoke of Westminster Cathdral.

> Lo, in yon brilliant window-niche
> How statue-like I see thee stand,
> The agate lamp within thy hand,
> Ah! Psyche, from the regions which
> Are holy land.

It was from Roland that I first heard the name of Gerard Manley Hopkins; whose few poems in *The Spirit of Man* he pointed out to me in the little copy of that book he gave me; a poet whom I was to hear later in Cambridge, but in terms how different. For Roland his poems were not 'literature' but words of power, living words, speaking from the heart of Newman's convert to the heart of a semblable and brother, a young man living a similar experience, feeling in himself the desire to go 'where springs not fail'. I, not feeling in myself any response to that call, trembled I think as one might on the edge of a cliff over which one does not wish to throw oneself. But how different—and how much closer to the heart of poetry—was Roland's response to Hopkins than the literary detachment of those Cambridge critics for whom the heart's blood of the poet was colourless, odourless and tasteless. As my grandparents had sung to me the songs of Scotland years before, as if speaking their own immediate feelings, so Roland spoke Hopkins's words as if his own; for they gave utterance to his own being. What a degradation of poetry it is, God knows, that any should dare to speak its words otherwise. The 'detachment' of criticism is something monstrous and perverted in comparison with that living utterance, spoken from life to life, and for the living of life. And should a poet set pen to paper who is not prepared to meet that test of speaking for any heart in a situation of vital need of words to give form to some crisis of the life? The critics turn into a dead language the most living language of all; and I am glad that my first encounter with Hopkins's poetry was of a living kind.

The story, then, resumes again when—was it a year after our separation? I do not remember, nor does it matter— when, in the time such events take to ripen, Roland's father came to plead with mine that we be allowed to meet again; for his son had gone into a monastery with the intention of becoming a monk. Not, as it proved, Rome after all; he had so far compromised with his father's strong prejudices as to become an 'Anglo-Catholic'. My father shared Mr. Haye's sense of the gravity of this new threat to the ignorant and narrow sect to which piety towards their ancestors bound them. Perhaps too the continued misery of his daughter

149

inclined my father to lift a ban imposed, as he by now must have seen, too late to undo the harm from which he would have saved me if he could: the harm and pain of sexual awakening. The forces of attack now were more powerful than the demon Eros; the Blessed Virgin and all the saints were a threat more to be feared; 'Mariolatry', as it was called. So it came about that at the end of the school term in which I sat my London Matriculation examination I found myself travelling in the Cornish Riviera Express in a corner seat, with Mrs. Haye and Ernest opposite and little Charity curled on my knee. Mr. Haye was to follow for his brief fortnight a few days later; and Roland. I was happy because I was to see him again, and because our parents were no longer enemies.

The village of Gwithian, not far from Hale, was still, in those days, Cornish. That Celtic race, who felt themselves more akin to the Bretons than to the English, and whose language had died within living memory, were still fighting off the invasion of English summer visitors; money, then, was not the supreme value. Two English maiden ladies who had called their house 'Apple Orchard', and who took summer guests, were persecuted until they left; their laundry would be cut to ribbons on their clothes-line during the night, and the like. Mr. Haye saw himself as the returning native, not the alien invader: and I, a Scottish Separatist at heart, warmed to this race who were making a last stand for Merlin's land, Avalon and the Grail. Among those deep lanes of vervain and marjoram and harts-tongue ferns, where glow-worms shone in the dusk, I felt clean of Ilford. It was Roland's father, I think, whom I really loved; he who treated me always with old-fashioned courtesy, and who loved Hardy as I did. Roland's more urbane literary tastes were, truth to say, beyond my scope; but Mr. Haye's longing to return to his roots was like my own. I smoked my first cigarette with charming Ernest (who went to the Merchant Taylor's School, a 'public school', and who already had the manner of 'a gentleman') in the coign of a cliff between highland and lowland, basking not in tragedy but in the summer sun.

When Roland at last arrived I discovered that I was out of my depth; his fantasies had raced ahead, nourished on books I had not read, drawn from sources unguessed by me. He arrived with characteristic panache, with a rosary ever in his pocket or his hand, and sandals on his bare feet. From me he averted his eyes, to me he addressed no word. I was no longer, it seemed, his lyric love, but temptation itself, the poison apple, the gate of hell. How near young tragedy lies to comedy, comedy to tragedy! But in retrospect I do not laugh, for the tragedy—Roland's not mine—seems to me now both other and greater than I thought it then. Then the tragedy seemed to me our poor broken dreams of love; now, I see a youth struggling to free himself from the underworld, hindered by those who might have helped him, thrown back, after each attempt to escape, into his prison. The sandals and the monk's habit were a last desperate disguise by whose means he hoped to elude his captors. Easy enough to laugh at that pose of mock-mediaevalism, but now I see in all Roland's metamorphoses something heroic, the attempt to impose a style, a form, upon his life in an environment which knew nothing of style or form; an affirmation of the imagination in a world formless, narrow and commonplace. The failure was no less tragic than inevitable; for a style is not to be created in a day by those who inherit none. No doubt the mock-mediaevalism has lent a style to many a young man in like circumstances; and Roland's fine new talk of vestments and ceremonial—so contemptible to my father for whom the embarrassing 'sincerity' of the uncultured working-class Methodists seemed (and was, if Gibbon is to be believed) nearer to the Christianity of the slaves of the Roman catacombs than the civilized and civilizing order of the Catholic religion—expressed a deep nostalgia for human culture, for all that rises above the surface of the bog of animality which we all carry in ourselves, the subsistence level of barbarism which for ever breeds its own effortless kind.

Protestantism—considered as religion, not as social reform—has ever been the blind protest of ignorance against a knowledge beyond its ken; and those who outgrow its narrow notions can but leave its sects; a breaking, inevitably, of family and social ties which may be as damaging to those who go as to those who stay. Within Catholic Christendom, the most ignorant and the most learned, the simplest faith and the most subtle metaphysical understanding rest upon the same mythology, the same liturgy, the same words and signs and symbols. Only the Catholic Church sends (or, in those days, sent) down its emissaries into all places: the civilizing reach of the Church was indeed universal, and Roland's first instinct was doubtless right, to take sanctuary in Westminster Cathedral. Perhaps after the initial shock his father would have minded no more than his son's becoming an Anglican; for he lost him in any case. But John Wesley had been a member of the Church of England, and for an Englishman it is the Church of his ancestors, his language, and the specifically English cultural inheritance. By entering the Orders of the Anglican Church perhaps Roland also hoped to overleap the barrier of class and to mix as an equal with men who shared his taste and knowledge, so far above his station. Taste, even more than knowledge: for Roland had taste. The numberless Noakeses of the universities can absorb unlimited information and remain their own crude selves; but Roland's case was different, by nature he was a man of culture, but born in exile.

Roland had passed out of my ken; but in my young grief I thought only 'Why does he not love me any more? How have I deserved this?' Once, in the kitchen of the cottage, I found myself for a moment alone with him. I thought myself a very Marguerite of injured love, and stretched out

152

my hands to him, I seem to remember, in silent pleading; but he left the room murmuring 'It is the Triple Vow, the Triple Vow'. Dressed still in the literary wardrobe of Huysmans and Patrice de la Tour du Pin, Roland was now a fugitive. In bringing me to Cornwall as a luring-bird to retrieve their Hound-of-Heaven-hunted son, Roland's parents failed and saw me fail. No longer his lyric love, I was a little schoolgirl who had just passed her matriculation examination and who must now decide whether, in the sixth form, she would take 'arts' or 'science'.

How artlessly I played my part without my Svengali I realize as I recall the only notion which entered my head as appropriate to the grief and bewilderment I then felt. I knew that a mile or two along the cliff road towards Portreath there was a steep cliff above rocks which the beautiful green and purple waters moiled in a pool called Hell's Mouth. I chose a beautiful spot for my suicide; for suicide in a spot so beautiful seemed an ending worthy of the dream we had woven. I ran from the cottage, tears streaming from my eyes as I hurried along the cliff-road on a summer evening of perfect beauty; reciting, as I ran, all the poetry I knew. I was miserable enough, to be sure, but only miserable, this time, as a schoolgirl of fifteen. The real mutilation had been the earlier one, when my father had shattered, with such violence, the archetypal flower of love. A few days before I had been happy just because there were flowers and glow-worms in the hedges of Avalon. I had, besides, seen Roland's bony pimpled body for the first and last time in my life, as he bathed with his brother in a certain very beautiful pool among the rocks; and I had shuddered. Such a body was best hidden by a brown habit tied with a girdle of rope knotted thrice. But how face a future without our dreams, without that 'someday', that painted paradise we had built together? So I rushed along that cliff road in childish tears, declaiming

Treacherous in calm, and terrible in storm,
Who shall put forth on thee,
Unfathomable sea?

—feeling that words so beautiful must fit my condition. I lingered above Hell's Mouth where in the moiling waters the seaweed was purple in the green, uncertain now I had reached the here and now to which I had so fancifully conducted myself, what to do. So I lingered by the place weeping for a while, before I was ignominiously led back by two non-conformist clergymen who happened to be passing. I do not think I would have either jumped or fallen over the cliff if they had not come; but there must have been silly children who have been less sure-footed or more desperate than I was.

Nothing ended cleanly or clearly; Roland gave up the Triple Vow and returned to Kings' College in the Strand, I think with some grant, to read Theology and become an Anglican clergyman; and we were allowed to meet. He talked to me much of religion but I remember nothing of it; phrases like the 'via media' that gave a new style to his speech suggest to me now that he had been reading Newman. Only one image stands clear; the image of a Roman Missal which Roland gave me. In it he wrote, in that backhand I remember so well, 'To my wife'; reverting to our old plighted troth. One day my father discovered the book; and I opened it to find those words cut out, deeply cut through many pages of the fine India-paper. The savage wound the blade of my father's penknife made in the pages cut something from my soul; something he cut out, once and forever. Marriage, certainly, it has since seemed, has never been possible for me.

I remember my virgin self, on the far side of that blasting of first love, looking down the long sweet vista of a woman's destiny. I remember standing, one day, on the edge of a field of hay-grass, wild roses in the hedge, birds singing, and

such heavy richness of love on me that I felt myself transfigured by my womanhood into something more sacred
than my mere self. It is the sense of the sacredness of sexual
love that I chiefly remember; and once, I remembered
Roland told me of a girl who had accosted him; a prostitute.
I had not heard of prostitutes until that moment; 'I was
sorry for that girl', I remember Roland saying; but as for
myself, such a pang went through my heart that sex could
ever be so degraded from what I knew it to be, from what
our young love knew it to be, the very altar of life, that I
pressed my wounded heart with my hand and was speechless with pity and grief. I grieved for days, for ever, feeling
in that moment the full distance between what sexual love
was meant to be, as in Eden, to use the symbols of that old
myth, and what it is in the bitter world of Experience. It
seems no less terrible to me now; to the poet who still
remembers Eden, long after the woman has left its fields.

Mine, I think, was the normal response of woman, considered as a human and not as an animal being; the 'norm'
being a lost human perfection and not the mean or average,
which may, unfortunately, be very different. Yet I wonder
if every woman in love does not see, as my childish self then
saw, with pity and shame and grief the distances we can
wander from the perfection all seek but few find in *amor*.
Like a maiden in a tapestry field of flowers I for a time found
it; my first love was, in its way, an epiphany; an epiphany
of human love as it was in the first earthly Paradise.

The magic of first love faded in the changing pattern of
our lives. Roland the theological student found new inter-
ests and, at last, new friends of the kind he needed most.
A distinguished rising Anglican theologian, who was at that
time Vicar of Ardeley, befriended him, and he went often
for weekends to a vicarage of which he used to speak with
the gratitude of a lost traveller who has reached at last a
green isle in his storm-tossed voyage. He was invited to take
me, one weekend; his lyric love, to be scrutinized by these

friends from the world of true culture, the world we had known must exist—for had we not lived upon its images in poetry and in music—but to which we did not belong. Roland was beginning to hope to belong. I went with him— it was autumn, and the hedges were golden and bright red bryony berries trailed among the thorns—and was for the first time a guest in the house of cultured people.

Everything there seemed to me as beautiful, as perfect, as the bedroom of little Miss Ellie seemed to Tom the chimney-sweep. I could not have said what the indefinable differences were between this house and any I had known. These rooms were not much larger than those of West View, yet there was a dimension in them which ours lacked; the dimension of culture, of mental spaces, of which the many books, the blue china, the grand piano were but the outward signature. I did not understand, then, that the windows, which seemed to me so simple and so right, as those of the manse had also seemed, were so not through size but through proportion, through a mathematical secret knowledge. The vicar's wife seemed to me as beautiful as Gwen Ffrangçon-Davies herself, in *The Immortal Hour* and she sang carols with Latin and French in them, old and lovely cadences that spoke to my imagination as if they were sung by Botticelli's angels. Why was this old furniture (in Ilford 'new' furniture was what everyone admired and wished to possess), the plain linen covers, the simple curtains, so subtly and indefinably right? Qualitative differences which I could not define, I felt. I sensed values I did not understand; I did not judge but felt myself judged, and, like Tom the chimney-sweep, knew myself for an uncouth little ape. Yet, like that same Tom, I loved the beauty in whose light I stood condemned. I was speechless with gauche shyness, and cowered beside Roland on a sofa while the vicar played and his wife sang 'Lullay, Lullay thou little tiny child', and 'I sing of a maiden that is makeless'. Precious, it may be; but to Roland and to me a spring of pure water in our desert.

It was not that the vicar or his wife snubbed me, but that I knew myself wanting by their values. Roland, seeing me in that context, must, with his fastidious eye, have seen it too. How could they have known who or what was still enfolded in the scale-leaves of my young bud? I did not know myself; or if I did, could not have told. They could not have known, even, how beautiful I thought were their house, their rooms, their blue china bowls of autumn berries, their music and their gleaming old oak chests and their books. I knew myself judged and condemned, of course; but by myself. I did not think myself worthy to set foot in their house or their company, because it was quite evident to me that I was not. They saw Roland's *kore* smelling of Hades, but did not know how I mourned in that prison-house. They may have advised Roland—rightly, indeed—not to encumber his future by an engagement with a girl of the Hades from which he hoped to escape; I should advise the same in a like case. So after that humiliating glimpse of a perfection which judged and condemned me, he became, I think, a little more aloof.

But the end, after all, was a dramatic victory for my father. At the time of the General Strike, students of London University volunteered to drive buses and underground trains, and an enjoyable time they must have had. Roland volunteered for the underground, and wrote to tell me of his adventures. But in my father's house the General Strike was viewed very differently. My father hoped passionately for the victory of the strikers; his two brothers, coal-miners, were involved, and all his loyalty was to his people and to their cause. Such was his fervour that he carried me with him; I thought myself then, for the first and last time in my life, an ardent Socialist, reflecting my father's strong feelings without really understanding them, or knowing, myself, the world of the working class. My mother, with her country roots, and her Scottish pride, naturally shrank, as I did, from crowds and from the proletariat in instinctive aversion from their alien smell. I had seen mean and smelly back-yards and dirty children when visiting my father's brothers, but felt no kinship as with my mother's people. Yet I wrote to Roland an indoctrinated socialist letter telling him that he and his like were the enemies of the cause of the people. He was very much piqued and seized upon the pretext of telling me that we had better stop seeing one another. He was right; for had I not chosen my father rather than my lover?

To console me my parents gave me a tiny box-room as a study; I could furnish it as I liked. I had bookshelves, and an old oak writing-table with a leather top; rather a nice table. But the walls were peacock blue and the curtains of orange velvet, a hideous colour-scheme fashionable at the time. My poor mother also turned out of my bedroom my old white painted chest-of-drawers and the faded flowery cre-tonne curtains behind which my clothes had hung.all these years, and my little white-painted iron bedstead, and the old wooden toy-cupboard, and gave me a hideous new bed-room suite from Harrison Gibson's furniture stores in inlaid mahogany veneer, with sombre mirrors that swallowed up the soul into the lonely prisons of Ilford's coldest hells, reflecting themselves for ever and ever. Yet she meant it kindly, and I did not myself know why these gifts, which had cost her so much, and which I tried to see as wonderful improvements, clenched my heart in a vice of misery and the sense of all hope lost. It was called 'ingratitude'; but if I was cruel, I too suffered.

At the time, and for twenty years after, I thought it impossible to imagine suffering greater than I underwent in those years, in that episode; but now I understand that, but for Roland, I might never have escaped the prison-house. I was fledged for freedom now; Roland had helped me to sever every cord of attachment that held me to that under-world. He had shown me images of intellectual beauty, icons of that perfection for which I might have longed in

vain if I had not been put in possession of the keys of freedom, the books and the music he first made known to me.
Once these seemed only the adornments of love; now that
love is remembered, rather, as an initiation into the music
of Chopin. As for Roland, he too had been given his chance
of freedom. Through what experiences his way led him
before his early death, I do not know; but I hope that for
him not all was lost illusions.

CHAPTER FOUR

Here I was Happy

'What might have been is an abstraction
Remaining a perpetual possibility
Only in a world of speculation.'

OR ME France has been that perpetual possibility,
never realized, but on several significant occasions
offering me the choice I did not take; mistakenly, it
might be said, for on each occasion the French alternative
has been manifestly the better; if better and worse are to be
assessed in any terms but the imponderable difference
between what is, and what is not, on our way, woven into
the pattern of our fate, willed for us by God, or however
else one may phrase it. Hardly ever have I wondered, about
France, was that the right way I did not take? It might have
led me by a very beautiful and enriching detour. I have
noticed whenever anyone, friend or stranger, has described
to me some significant choice or action in life, they have
concluded by saying, 'But what else could I have done?'
Nothing else; so we always reply, can only reply; another
person might have acted very differently, but that particular
'I'? We act as we must, being what we are.

The beginning of France was before the end of Roland,
but I find it possible only to follow the separate threads, not
to disentangle chronological order, long forgotten. Chrono-
logy has little to do with recollection, which raises up
wholes, like separate poems, beautifully coherent and complete. Yet there are strange modulations of theme, not
recognized at the time; and only years later did I wonder if

an unknown Englishman who carved, in a little sunny cave on one of the sandy beaches of Le Pouldu, the words 'Here I was happy' had been Dowson, his heart at that moment no more sick of an old passion than was mine when I read those words. It was not so very long after he had lived at Le Pouldu, after all, that I followed; for are not poets and painters only the first arrivals of the succeeding swarm? It is bitter, but salutary, for even poets to remember that they carry the infection of the civilization from which they are running to the places to which they run; we leave our intangible litter in the lives of those amongst whom we live.

Yet when I first saw those little secret rocky coves, and the mistletoe-fringed Laïta, and the old cities of Quimper and Quimperlé, the destruction (in which, as part of the influx of alien presences, I played my insignificant part) was not yet apparent to the eye. The maids at our little hotel still wore their beautiful dignified costume; high coifs fluttering with starched bands; a little different in every village, and the essential quality of the beauty of each girl enhanced, not effaced, by the identity of her black dress and a ribboned coif worn 'with a difference'. The little coves and sandy beaches were still secluded and scarcely visited, and only a few of the houses as yet belonged to summer visitors from Paris. We came to visit Le Pouldu through a series of circumstances which deeply affected the course of my life. My father was the agent, yet now I think of it he seems to have been chiefly instrumental on my behalf, and to have benefited very little for himself, though that perhaps through no fault of mine.

My father and mother had spent a fortnight, during a summer vacation, at a teachers' conference held at Girton; a rare emergence, for my father, from the company of his inferiors into that of educated people. There he made one of the few friendships I ever remember him to have formed, with one of the lecturers at the conference, a distinguished teacher of English at a famous school in Paris, who later rose

161

high in the Ministère d'Instruction Générale. M. d'H—'s particle was not, like poor Roland's, a fiction, but inherited from his father, a landowner who had been, so he told us the story, defrauded of his estates by a dishonest factor. I remember he once said, in passing, that the particle would have opened for him 'many doors in Paris' which he did not care to open; and in retrospect I marvel at how little realization I then had of social differentiation or those things upon which it rests; for it seemed to me perfectly natural that he should prefer to converse with my father and myself on English poetry rather than with ducs or marquis on nothing in particular; a very brash opinion, as I now see. But at that time (daughter and grand-daughter of school masters and school ma'ams) I had the notion that education was the only thing that mattered, and that to be 'clever' was more honourable than to be nobly-born.

I have since known a few members even of the aristocracy and it has slowly dawned on me that the reason why the well-bred are not necessarily well-educated, and often seem to find great difficulty with their spelling (at first this surprised and amused me, product as I am of an excellent secondary school and university education) is that when you are the thing itself you do not need to read about it in books. An education comes from books, but a culture is transmitted, in countless imponderable ways, by the people amongst whom we live. Much literature is a mere substitute for direct access to a society with its *mores*, and the richnesses and subtleties of a world where individual consciousness and social relationships are more fully developed than in the Ilfords of the world.

But if I had no realization of how M. d'H came to be what he was, I did recognize his quality. He was—apart from my one miserable weekend at the vicarage of Ardeley—the first person of culture I had met. As a child I had known, however meagrely, participation in the songs and legends of my Scottish birthright; but these stories of places and per-

162

sons whose names in Scotland endear them to the singers of their fame by their nearness, in Ilford could not help my mother, still less myself, to live our lives, but only remind us of our remoteness from the places of our ancestors and from those banks and braes of heather and broom, the deer and the laverock, to which the imagination of the race is wedded. In M. d'H I recognized something at once novel and familiar, an attitude, a relationship with French and European civilization of the same nature, though on a higher cultural level, as my fast fading participation in my Border birthright.

I saw him for the first time in the drawing-room of our house, standing against the French window, casting a kind of light in the room. He seemed too big for the house. He was not, perhaps, exceptionally tall, but, as at Ardeley the very tables and book-cases seemed to have an added and intangible dimension, so did M. d'H seem not to be contained in the familiar rooms. The presence of this fair Frenchman with his flashing blue eyes and ironic smile, seemed at once to require, and to affirm, spaces of interior freedom my father's house did not provide. Not only did the rooms, the spindly drawing-room furniture, the dining-table and the side-board with its mahogany knobs and brackets and bevelled pieces of mirror seem suddenly small and cramped and crowded, but so did the accepted values of the house; all, that is, except literature, about which he and my father, schoolmasters both, talked in complete accord. I saw my father, for once, in the company of a man of culture; and wished with all my heart that he could be so always. But it was characteristic of him that, during the war, he refused to apply for any promotion, for the headmastership of a school, because he would not use the advantage of his position as a civilian to steal an advantage on men at the war. All my father is in that; his unworldly idealism, but also his colossal pride in taking always the lowest place. I had not then read Plato's words about idleness—that not only

163

are those idle who are not employed, but who might employ their talents better—but I felt always that my father wasted his abilities through inverted pride. Very likely I was as wrong by his standards as he seemed by mine.

It was as if my father permitted himself to rise to his full stature only at a remove; when he spoke of Shelley and Coleridge and Wordsworth, he judged them in terms of their own values; yet he lived by those of the Wesleyan Methodists, whose values for him represented a norm above which he might perhaps soar, sometimes, in thought, but which remained, like sea-level, that from which he took his bearings. He was no less aware than I was of the cultural meagreness and general ignorance of the Methodists but as Blake says of Swedenborg (to whom also Protestant clergy represented a norm) 'A man carried a monkey about for a show, and because he was a little wiser than the monkey, grew vain . . .'—a constant danger when the norm is abnormal. My father's monkeys were so far below M. d'H's horizon that for him they were non-existent. I am interpreting in retrospect what I then felt simply as a quality of his presence, a mental spaciousness he brought with him, and in which I too began to feel my wings. He waded like Gulliver among our gimcrack furniture, both tangible and mental. Later he used to describe to me his own education by the Oratorians; the splendours and grandeurs of the Catholic liturgy. He would chant, in his fine voice, those majestic and ancient processional hymns of Holy Week, and describe the Tenebrae and the Vigil and the rite of the Paschal candle, bound by unbreakable bonds of love to the Church in whose doctrines he no longer believed. A year or two later, he took me, on Easter day, to Mantes Cathedral; torturing himself with a beauty he loved but felt himself compelled to reject. My father was I think pained to see his own religion of 'simple faith' swept aside as not for a moment worthy of consideration, let alone comparison with the Catholic faith; held, by the monkeys, to be an idolatrous and superstitious

164

ignorance lingering unaccountably in 'backward' countries like France, Spain, Italy and Ireland. My father encountered in his distinguished friend a respect and devotion for everything about the Catholic Church and its culture and its priests except the one point of agreement my father found in it—the truth of its central teaching and the divinity of its Founder. To him, no less than to any Jesuit, Dominican, Benedictine or Oratorian, the little Protestant sects dear to my father were heresies of the ignorant.

Were there, then, really such men in the world? Or a world in which men were like him? Roland and I had scarcely known enough even to envisage such a possible world. To meet such a man in my father's house was, for me, as if an angelic liberator had come with a key; yet it was all so simple, my liberation, with no battle at all, just the disappearance of the battlefield, which had suddenly become small and remote; even on that single visit M. d'H made to our house (he never again consented to return among that cramping physical and mental furniture) I sensed freedom.

When first he saw me, so he later told me, coming in by the French window where my mother's tubs of blue agapanthus were in flower, he was wonder-struck to find in that wingless underworld such a being as myself. M. d'H was, I think, the first human being (except my mother) who ever saw who I was; and that is something far more precious than what the young call 'love'. Between us, in the first exchanged look, there was the mutual recognition of beings of the same species, the same race, who meet in an alien world. I knew instantaneously that this was, for me, a meeting of marvellous promise and inestimable value; a meeting of the imagination, as if with Coleridge himself. (M. d'H had written a book on Coleridge, whom of all English poets he most admired, and with whose marital miseries he most deeply sympathized.) He became, from that visit, my first teacher, to whom I gave the reverence and love of a disciple.

He loved to teach; to him, the communication of knowledge gave, it seemed, as much pleasure as it gave me to absorb it.

He never returned; but he invited my father most pressingly to spend his summer holiday at Le Pouldu.

The first summer holiday after my meeting with Roland had been spent in the company of very different mentors. Two or three Wesleyan Ministers had set up little wooden holiday bungalows on a stretch of shingle on the south coast, near a Martello tower, which one of them had bought, but not yet converted into a house. There my father was invited to bring his family; and he, my mother and I all slept in one bell-tent, and cooked on a primus stove. This I did not mind, nor the stretch of shingle (which that year became famous for a peculiarly sordid sex-murder), where grew strange maritime plants, which spoke to the botanist in me. But in the company of these Ministers and their families I chafed in cramped mental spaces and longed only to get out, out. These Ministers were the best mentors my father could produce as influences to bring his daughter to that 'conversion' which he felt that I, on the verge of womanhood, ought to undergo. Sudden conversions make up the romance of the story of John Wesley's preachings on village greens and outside those churches he was banned from entering; and I think Dinah Morris was probably my father's favourite female character in fiction; after Shakespeare's Portia, perhaps, or Cordelia. These dramatic shifts of consciousness were considered to be the mark of true religion; and indeed Jung has since, in psychological terms, written of the same kind of re-orientation. But to me nothing of this kind happened. Instead, one of those wearers of celluloid dog-collars, of peculiar physical coarseness, fell furtively in love with me; and another, a man of some spiritual stature, I saw tethered, like Coleridge, by a 'coarse domestic life' and beset, besides, by young women of his congregation pining with repressed sexual

166

desire under the spell of a magnetic physical charm he seemed unable to control. So, taking refuge on the flat roof of the Martello tower, I wrote daily replies to Roland's daily letters (in one a long Proustian description of white water-lilies floating on a still stream; so strangely do certain images emerge at certain times. Long after it was among the letters Roland, at my father's request, returned to me; he did not, of course, return all; but I was hurt that he returned my first exercise in the literary art, for I had taken pains with that piece of fine writing), read the first volumes of *The Golden Bough*, Jane Harrison, and Gilbert Murray's Euripides; all lent me by Roland. I found in the archaic religions a world infinitely more satisfying to my imagination, and my own long thoughts blended and intertwined with cloud and sea and sky undefiled by the stifling human community below. I kept myself proudly apart, reciting to myself Keats and Swinburne. Perhaps my resolute aloofness was a challenge, for the Ministers all in turn by persuasion, pleading and flattery tried to capture me; but it could no more be done than, according to Swedenborg, spirits of different qualities can remain in one another's societies. I knew with the absolute certainty of instinct that I was not of their kind, as a blackbird knows it is not a starling. On the roof of my tower I felt myself protected by the spirits of the poets and by the ancient gods. My father perhaps saw that my books were better company, and let me be.

But in Brittany it was I who, for the first time since Bavington, was in my element, my father out of his. We were only able to afford a holiday really beyond our means and above our station because the rate of exchange that year had made France accessible to the English lower middle class; and we were but three drops in a tidal wave which poured in. There was even, at Le Pouldu, another family from Ilford, a sandy-haired spectacled boy from my father's school, and his parents. My father, who in the world of the d'H—s and their friends felt, I think, as unprotected and exposed as M. d'H had felt submerged and hampered in Ilford, sought them out, finding relief in his habitual role of doing good to his inferiors rather than taking pleasure in the company of his equals. To me these people were a humiliating reminder, with their faint cockney voices, of Ilford, which I would have liked to forget into the same non-existence as it had for the d'H—'s. My father, who had called me 'uncharitable' towards the Wesleyans of the Martello tower now called me uncharitable because I would have nothing to do with these (as it seemed to me) underworld people who had followed us up from Hades into the sunlight of France which shone so marvellously for me. Perhaps he was right; but it is not easy for the living to escape from the world of the dead, and it seems to me still that winged souls are more often dragged down by the commonplace herd who, ignorant of the use of wings, clip them and forbid their flight, than the wingless injured by the escape of the winged ones. Who, among the vulgar, heeds the misery of imagination hampered and thwarted? The question of charity cannot be resolved in these terms, nor can talent best 'serve humanity' by renouncing its vocation. To evade a high task by seeking refuge in a low one is not humility but despair, spiritual sloth, even a kind of inverted pride.

But my father handed me over willingly enough to M. d'H who, from the first, addressed his discourse chiefly to me, glad that I should have this opportunity of improving my French, and of otherwise benefiting from the educational company of the distinguished schoolmaster.

So in aromatic woods, and on cliffs trembling in the haze of Monet's paintings, and on the river Laïta, and in the old streets of Quimperlé, and on the sand-dunes of Morbihan, I rambled with my wonderful mentor and his two little sons in a world apart, while on the *plage* my mother learned the art of filet embroidery from Mme d'H—. He discoursed on the habits of birds, as he watched kingfisher, woodpecker

168

and jay; heard me repeat whole memorized pages of Michelet on birds over and over again until my pronunciation pleased his exacting ear; philosophized, as Frenchmen will, on Shelley's view of love, of Renan's view of Christianity, of the cruelty of nature (exemplified in the lives of insects, reptiles and even his beloved birds) incompatible with the belief in a beneficent god. Humanism is a poor philosophy, but at the time he broke for me, cobweb by cobweb, the religious snare in which I had become so agonizingly entangled. As my wings were freed I began to feel again, for the first time since my lost childhood, the strength of my own spirit. With the blithe thoughtlessness of youth I imagined that now I had come into my own, now my long imprisonment was over, now the bright sun would shine on me for ever.

I suppose my mentor spoiled me, for he abetted my rebellion; he saw it as a matter of course that I must get away from Ilford; made me feel that I belonged with the happy few, with Coleridge, with Shelley, with such as he himself was. In his company it did not seem like a flight or a rebellion but like an awakening from some gloomy dream. I had no uncharitable thoughts towards the people of Hades, I only wished to be with those of my own kind; and did not need to be convinced by argument that the beaten road

> Which those poor slaves with weary footsteps tread
> Who travel to their home among the dead
> By the broad highway of the world

was not for me; with him I felt no sense of guilt for being what I was. Nor can I find, if I search my conscience, that the immortal judges have had cause to reproach me for vanity or pride, then or since, but rather for continual doubt and discouragement and evasion of their summons. Over and over again I have been misled by listening to the voices of the world, to my father's voice, persuading me not to listen to my daimon but to devote myself to the routine of lower duties. I have never been able to use my wings but when I could elude my father's moral values, admirable values for those who walk, but irrelevant when I have sought to fly. Perhaps I was a spoiled and selfish only child who expected the indulgence from the world which my mother had given me: yet I accepted my destiny, after all, at a price of suffering which many would be reluctant to pay. Suffering follows automatically for those who take it upon themselves to undergo in full consciousness the experiences of life which happen, indeed, to all, but which the instinct of self-protection induces those whom Blake calls 'sleepers' and Shelley 'the dead' to put from their minds.

Ilford, considered as a spiritual state, is the place of those who do not wish to (or who cannot be) fully conscious, because full consciousness would perhaps make life unendurable. What if some Mr. and Mrs. should wake to find that they are strangers to one another's souls? What if some ambition, 'forgotten', like Roland's doctor's overall, should stir too painfully into consciousness the desire for some skill or craft or knowledge inaccessible? If the corpse buried in the trim little back garden were to be resurrected into anguished life, the poor weak weeping ugly disgraceful Lazarus would only have to be killed and buried once more. The phrase which describes the state of those who 'cannot call their souls their own' is not without truth, and often for social and economic reasons which are beyond the control of the sufferers. To break up a marriage, however soul-destroying, money is needed; to become a doctor or a scholar costs money; and the sensibility of an artist or a poet cannot grow in a mean underworld, and in solitude. It is no wonder that in the Ilfords there are more who fear than who desire the stirrings of consciousness. For one who escapes, many more must be thrown back to suffer in a prison-house made only more intolerable by every glimpse of the world of unattainable freedom.

Brittany was, for me, a mountain-top from which I was shown, for the first time, the world; and I drank deep draughts of ecstatic happiness. My life, from there, seemed a winged flight, like that of Michelet's birds. '*Rêves ailées, ravissements de nuit, si vous étiez, pourtants. Si vraiment vous viviez!*'—so I incanted my soaring aspiration, so M. d'H summoned me to rise to my destiny, or flattered a child's vanity, as may be. For one thing I am above all grateful: he had the generosity to hope, to wish for me a winged destiny. That is a kind of love very different from turbid *amor*, such as poor Roland had laid at the feet of the object of his desire and subject of his dreams. For M. d'H I really was 'half angel and half bird', for he believed me winged, and summoned me to flight. In the Virgin blue, hands folded in prayer, who looks always downwards, beholding only the upturned face of her child, whose image Roland adored, I never saw an icon of my own soul; but in M. d'H's bird-winged race I did, and secretly rejoiced.

The difference between those lives in Hades and the life I now saw being lived on all sides was not a matter of being materially richer, or, indeed, of being happier. The ability to live in, not merely to live through the present, implies a kind and quality of consciousness, which is, like Blake's little flower, 'the labour of ages'; and is not this to have a culture? In Ilford all was provisional, was an 'interim', for the time being, would 'do well enough for now'. This view of life was implicit also in my father's non-conformist religion, other-worldly rather than sacramental. To my father himself the poets he loved seemed dwellers in an Elysium remote from his own world. Shelley's blue Mediterranean and Baeae's bay, Browning's gondolas, even Tennyson's Victorian flower-gardens were as remote as Eden or Xanadu. In the world of Scottish songs and border-ballads, the life which nourished the poetry was the very life the poetry celebrated and enhanced; the poetry wedded, in Yeats's phrase, the imagination of the race to the land;

whereas in Ilford poetry brought not peace but a sword. But here again, in France, I sensed a culture in which the arts were a flower of the quality of life, and life nourished by the arts. M. d'H was far from happy; his marriage was a battlefield and he spared himself no whit of insight into its complex miseries; but his actual circumstances he regarded, and used, as the instrument, the keyboard and strings, from which he must evoke the full gamut of experience, explore, like Coleridge himself, the mysteries of the soul, its joy and its suffering.

In the Catholic peasant world of Brittany I sensed the same actuality, on a lower octave; the priest blessing the sea from the fishing-boats, the ex-voto tablets in the chapel of some local St. Barbe, bore witness to a spirituality not relegated to an after-life; here the miraculous was a dimension of the here and now, the bread and the wine and the fish in the sea, and no village so small but that some saint in Heaven was its especial guardian. The concreteness of painted madonna and wooden child, the candle-flames of prayer, embodied everywhere the Christian mysteries.

I knew that to write poetry in, from, or for Ilford was impossible; but I was too intent upon escape to ask myself the question, 'from what, and for whom, do you expect to be a poet?'.

Ought I to be ashamed, in retrospect, that I took my escape so lightly? I walked on air upon those cliffs whose irridescent envelope of light Monet painted. I saw sun and shadow swoon into Bonnard's mid-day trance, where Proust's *jeunes filles en fleurs* and Manet's shade their delicate flower-faces with little parasols. I stood dreaming in the shadow of old cathedrals, taking all as my due with no knowledge of the cost at which man has raised himself to the vision of such things. I was a little barbarian marvelling at a civilization whose price was beyond my ken.

To my regret and dismay I lost, within two years, my revered teacher; all was spoiled by his falling in love with me. I do not know whether in Brittany I had any inkling of this; if I had I put the unwelcome intuition from me. But when at Easter I was invited to stay in the château near Paris where he had at that time gone as headmaster to one of those new schools American millionaires were founding in England and France at the time, there was no evasion possible. All the pleasure of spring woods, of air heavy with the scent of chestnut flowers, of waking in a sunny bedroom to walk in glades blue with periwinkle, secluded from the multitude; of visiting the Opéra, of lunching with the millionaire himself in a house looking out upon the garden of M. Poincaré (yes, all these things I did) was spoiled by the intense embarrassment into which I was thrown by this unwanted love. In the spring woods my mentor had kissed me, and informed me that if and when he could free himself from his marriage, he would claim me. It seemed that he had not doubted my willingness; but his kiss filled me with a physical aversion which brought down all my edifice of admiration and friendship. It has often seemed to me since that the intrusion of sexual passion spoils all; and yet, only love casts those irridescent enchantments; had he not fallen in love with me, why should he have troubled with me? From that moment I longed only to escape his presence. I felt greatly to blame, wondering how I had incurred this miserable situation. I had lost, besides, the friend whom of all I had known I had most valued, who had opened my prison door and urged me to use my wings. Once more I was thrown back, confused and rebellious, upon Ilford, the lovely vistas of France closed to me; a spoiled and difficult young girl, now, the task of civilizing me which M. d'H had undertaken abandoned before it was well begun.